CHURCHILL, CRIPPS, AND INDIA
1939-1945

Pictorial Press Ltd.

SIR STAFFORD CRIPPS

CHURCHILL, CRIPPS, AND INDIA,
1939–1945

R. J. Moore

CLARENDON PRESS · OXFORD
1979

Oxford University Press, Walton Street, Oxford OX2 6DP

OXFORD LONDON GLASGOW
NEW YORK TORONTO MELBOURNE WELLINGTON
NAIROBI DAR ES SALAAM CAPE TOWN
KUALA LUMPUR SINGAPORE JAKARTA HONG KONG TOKYO
DELHI BOMBAY CALCUTTA MADRAS KARACHI

Published in the United States by
Oxford University Press, New York

British Library Cataloguing in Publication Data

Moore, Robin James
    Churchill, Cripps, and India, 1939–1945.
    1. India – Politics and government – 1919–1947
    I. Title
    320.9′54′035   JQ211   79–40188

ISBN 0–19–822485–0

Printed in Great Britain by
Butler & Tanner Ltd.,
Frome and London

PREFACE

THIS STUDY is part of a work that I began when the twentieth anniversary of Independence was approaching and India and Pakistan were at war. Since then Pakistan has itself become two nations, both unstable, while India has, by the resounding rejection of a new Empress governing by emergency powers, demonstrated a remarkable attachment to democracy. Thirty years after Independence there is, therefore, as much interest as ever in how it came to be that British policy-makers denied the principle of democratic self-determination in India until their own encouragement of the political mobilization of Muslims *qua* Muslims made unity impracticable.

The theme of this book is the long conflict over that principle between Sir Stafford Cripps, as the protagonist with Labour Party support, and Winston Churchill, as the colossus astride the War Cabinet, spokesman for Conservatism, and defender of the Empire.

The climax of the contest comes with Cripps's three-week mission to India in March–April 1942. In January, when he returned from being ambassador to Russia, Cripps basked in the reflected glory of the heroic defence of Leningrad and Moscow. He enjoyed popularity at a moment when Churchill's fortunes were low and sinking lower. British defeats in Malaya and Burma required that the War Cabinet be reconstructed, and that India's co-operation with the war effort be intensified. Cripps became a senior minister and at once addressed himself to the Indian problem. Against his long and fiercely held imperialist prejudices, Churchill was forced by the pressure of Cripps, his Labour colleagues, and the Americans to acquiesce in the offer of post-war Indian Independence and wartime association of the Indian parties with the central government. He allowed Cripps to leave for India with powers to negotiate a provisional national government. Aided by the like-minded

Viceroy, Lord Linlithgow, a reaction among his Conservative Cabinet colleagues, some desperate manœuvres of Cripps's, and a certain American hesitancy, Churchill was able at once to abort the negotiations and reduce a potentially serious rival.

The climactic events of the Cripps mission are anticipated by a battle of philosophies that reaches back into the 1930s. In an unpublished version of his memoirs Clement Attlee wrote:

I had a good many stiff contests with Churchill on India. It was a great surprise when he embraced the idea of the Cripps Mission. The lines on which Cripps was empowered to go went beyond anything previously considered by any Government. It embodied in fact some of the main ideas discussed by Cripps, Nehru and myself one weekend at Filkins.

The party at Cripps's country house in June 1938 marks the origin of the Cripps offer. It assembled in dissatisfaction at the National government's refusal to face the fact that as the dominant party of British India the Indian National Congress had just claims to early independence and participation in the central government. Official Conservative policy still sought to block such progress by a limited transfer of power to an all-India federation in which nominees of the princes and representatives of the Muslims would outweigh the Congress. Dissident Conservatives, led by Churchill, wanted no transfer of power at the centre whatever. Soon after the outbreak of war Cripps took the Filkins scheme to India. As a private Member of Parliament he sought, with Labour's goodwill, to effect *rapprochements* between Hindus and Muslims, and Congress and the British raj. Two Conservative Secretaries of State, Lord Zetland and L. S. Amery, urged the Filkins scheme upon Linlithgow and the Cabinet, until it finally emerged, mutilated almost beyond recognition by Churchill, as the August offer of 1940. The events of Cripps's first India visit, and the debates over the first offer, were a rehearsal for the contest of 1942.

The Cripps mission both suffered a failure and enjoyed a success that together gave it strategic importance for the largest transfer of power in modern times. The failure to set up a national government at the centre delayed full self-government, in Attlee's view, by some years; but, more significantly, it meant that a timely opportunity for Congress–Muslim League

co-operation was lost. Cripps offered Jinnah only the possibility
of a Muslim state of Pakistan, but in March 1942 that was sufficient to secure his co-operation. When Lord Wavell strove to
revive the Cripps offer, almost from the time of his appointment
as Viceroy in June 1943 until the Simla Conference two years
later, it was with the urgent sense that without the instrument
of central government to focus their joint attention on India's
problems Congress and the League were now drifting swiftly
towards separate nationhood. The mission's failure and the
consequent isolation of Congress from politics gave the League
three further years, beyond the early war years of Congress
non-co-operation, in which to capture the Muslim majority
provinces. By June 1945, when Churchill at length succumbed to
the need for a revival of the Cripps offer, Jinnah had etched
the writ of Pakistan so deep upon the Muslim consciousness
that he could defeat proposals for the central executive that
did not observe it.

The success of the mission was its guarantee of post-war
independence and a constitution made by Indians themselves.
As Cripps and Attlee had realized at the start of the war, the
terms of the old imperial relationship must give way to equality
between allies defending a common freedom. The necessity was
compounded by commercial, financial, and military realities.
The constitutional historian, Sir Reginald Coupland, recognized the release of the Cripps offer on 29 March 1942 as the
declaration of Indian independence. Once avowed, the
promise was never retracted; despite Congress preparations
for revolution in August 1942, it was reaffirmed as official
policy, finally to be honoured by the Labour governors of the
failing bank of Empire just five years later.

The larger work of which this study is a part concerns the
problem of freedom and unity in India from 1917 to 1947. In
an earlier book, *The Crisis of Indian Unity, 1917-1940* (Clarendon
Press, Oxford, and O.U.P., New Delhi, 1974), I emphasized the
interdependence of constitutional history and 'history from
below' for a complete understanding of the problem. Here I
am preoccupied with the implications of Britain's wartime
policies for the problem, but the approach is not intended to
imply that a lasting solution to India's political divisions was to
be found at the level of high politics. The full analysis of

British India's eventual achievement of independence as two nations also requires detailed studies in provincial development and Indian party politics. Nevertheless, *haute politique* may play the role of Marx's midwife.[1]

I wish to record my appreciation of the support of the study by funds administered by the Australian Research Grants Committee, the Smuts Managers (University of Cambridge), and the Study Leave and Research Committees of the Flinders University of South Australia. In the course of working on or towards this book I have enjoyed the hospitality of the Rockefeller Foundation at the Villa Serbelloni (Como), and of St. John's, Wolfson, and Selwyn Colleges, Cambridge. For making valuable manuscript sources available to me I am deeply indebted to Mr. Maurice Shock (for the Cripps–Wilson diary), Mr. Edward Milligan (for files of the Society of Friends), Professor J. Simmons (for R. G. Coupland's dairy), and the Alderman Library, University of Virginia (for Louis Johnson's papers). I have relied heavily upon the published volumes in the *Transfer of Power* series, superbly edited by Nicholas Mansergh, the late E. W. R. Lumby, and Sir Penderel Moon. It was my good fortune, while working in the relative isolation of Adelaide, to supervise Dr. Carl Bridge's study of 'The Conservative Party and All-India Federation, 1929–40', and at several points my text has been directed by his archival discoveries. Help with individual documents is acknowledged in the footnotes.

The Flinders University of South Australia   R. J. M.

[1] 'Force is the midwife of every old society pregnant with a new one.' *Capital* (Moscow, 1957), i. 751.

CONTENTS

ABBREVIATIONS USED IN THE NOTES

A.I.C.C.	All-India Congress Committee
C.D.	R. G. Coupland's Diary, India: 1941–1942, Rhodes House, Oxford
C.M.	*The Cripps Mission*, Vol. I of *The Transfer of Power*, H.M.S.O., 7 vols., 1970–77, eds. Nicholas Mansergh, E. W. R. Lumby, Penderel Moon
C.W.C.	Congress Working Committee
C.-W.D.	Diary kept by Cripps and Geoffrey Wilson, 1939–1940, in possession of Mr. Maurice Shock, Leicester University
F.R.U.S.	*Foreign Relations of the United States*, Washington
Home Pol.	Government of India Home Department Political series, Indian National Archives
I.C.G.	India Conciliation Group (papers at Friends' House, London)
I.N.A.	Indian National Archives, New Delhi
I.O.L.	India Office Library, London
J.N. Coll.	Jawaharlal Nehru Collection, Nehru Memorial Library, New Delhi
L/PO/1–	Private Office Papers series, India Office Library, London
Prem.	Prime Minister's Office files, P.R.O., London
P.R.O.	Public Record Office, London
Q.I.	*Quit India*, Vol. II of *Transfer of Power* series, as above
Z.C.	Zetland Collection, India Office Library, London

I

THE FIRST VISIT
(September–December 1939)

(i) The Sham Federation

WINSTON CHURCHILL condemned the India Act of 1935
as a 'monstrous monument of sham built by the pygmies'.[1] He
was not opposed to its provision making the provinces of
British India virtually self-governing, but to the scheme
linking their representatives with nominees of the Indian
princes in an all-India federation that was to have 'responsible'
government. His leadership of a diehard campaign against
the Conservative Party plan for a responsible federated India
chained him to the back-benches almost throughout the 1930s.
Though his antagonism to change in the central government
was misguided there was justice in his description of the
putative federation as a sham, glossing over the real obstacles
to Indian self-government.

The federal scheme was an eleventh-hour attempt to give
national coherence to political systems sharply contrasted and
communities deeply divided. A healing statute was to combine
some 560 principalities languishing under despotisms and
eleven provinces enjoying democratic institutions. The princes
would nominate a third of the members of the federal assembly.
The provincial legislatures would elect the rest, but the political
geography of the provinces made four of them predominantly
Muslim and the Muslims were guaranteed one-third of the
British Indian seats. The Indian National Congress, which

[1] B.B.C. broadcast, 29 Jan. 1935. The word 'sham' was misreported as 'shame'
in the published transcript (and so appears in Martin Gilbert's *Winston Churchill*, V
(1976), 595. Nicholas Mansergh had corrected the error in his *The Commonwealth
Experience* (1969), 267 and n.).

had claimed to speak for all of India during its two massive non-co-operation campaigns, might now at best win a third of the federal assembly seats, if it co-operated to work the Act.

The sham lay in the constitutional sleight of hand. Out of the discordant elements of India's political reality was conjured a fantasy of national harmony. One fallacy of the scheme, for example, was the assumption that the princes wanted federation, for the Act made it a condition that princes accounting for one half of the states' seats must sign instruments of accession. Neither before nor after the passing of the Act was there evidence for more than wishful thinking that the necessary number of princes would willingly yield any sovereignty to a federal authority. However, the crucial weakness of the scheme, as Attlee observed in Parliament, was its failure to accord to Congress an opportunity commensurate with its strength.

In February 1937, while the princes were being subjected to official blandishment, the provinces went to the polls. Congress won a victory that enabled it to form ministries in seven provinces. Whereas Congress had contested the elections in order to destroy the Act, the lure of office drew its provincial leaders into co-operation with the British government.

The scale of the Congress success induced insensitiveness to the interests of its political opponents. In the Congress provinces the Muslims lost the influence that they had enjoyed during the long years of non-co-operation. There political exclusion and the accession of new men to office gave rise to apprehensions. The Muslim imagination magnified insults into atrocities. In Uttar Pradesh, where Congress rejected as unnecessary a coalition with the Muslim League, the Governor, Sir Harry Haig, regarded such claims as fantastic. Certainly, Muslim grandees were affronted by the sudden invasion of silent secretariat corridors by curious Congress workers less than couth. They were also affected by tenancy legislation, just as in Bombay Muslim landholders suffered from a property tax and merchants from the introduction of prohibition. The old Liberal leader, Sir Chimanlal Setalvad, thought that Congressmen were drunk with victory, the Punjab Unionist Premier, Sir Sikander Hyat Khan, that they lost their heads.

It was not only that prominent Muslims were displaced,

that the spoils of office tended to flow along party lines, or that jubilation among Congress workers occasionally gave rise to violence at village level. There was also a strongly anti-Muslim thrust in Congress policy at the level of the High Command, the Working Committee, which sought to exercise a para-constitutional control over provincial governments. The latter were to hoist the Congress flag, sing the Congress anthem, and apply Gandhi's principles of education. Nehru launched a mass contact movement to win the support of poorer Muslims. The Governor of Bombay, Sir Roger Lumley, attested that there was genuine fear among the Muslims in his province, and Liaquat Ali Khan said that the same was true of Bihar.

By December 1937, the Secretary of State for India, Lord Zetland, was convinced that the strongest opposition to federation would come from the Muslims.[1] Their experience of provincial Congress rule would frighten them off participation in a federation to which Congress would be a party, albeit at truncated strength. The Muslim League, an insignificant organization at the time of the February elections, would be 'the dominant factor in determining the future form of the Government of India'.[2]

Muslim fears of Congress raj were exacerbated by the policy that Congress adopted towards the princes. In the name of self-determination for the states' peoples, the princes were enjoined to hold elections for the selection of their federal representatives. The policy not only reduced the likelihood of the princes' accession but, by destroying the balance of the paper federation, drove the Muslims to demand the revision of the constitution *de novo*. The sham was exposed.

Congress's electoral success of February 1937 and the High Command's subsequent policies ensured that the problem of India's constitutional advance would not be solved by the letter or the spirit of the Act designed by Churchill's despised pygmies. The Act fatally underestimated the strength of Congress, which would work its federal provisions only after violating its checks and balances. It afforded too little security

[1] Zetland to Linlithgow, 6 Dec. 1937, Zetland Collection (hereafter Z.C.), India Office Library.
[2] Zetland, *Essayez* (1956), 247.

for the princes or the Muslims to be drawn into its federation voluntarily.

While Churchill might feel vindicated in his judgement of the federal scheme as premature, as early as 1938 Labour Party leaders were already seeking a radical constitutional change, consistent with the proven importance of Congress.

(ii) The English Nehru

The week-end at Filkins to which Attlee traced the genesis of the Cripps offer[1] occurred at the beginning of Nehru's visit to England from June to October 1938. Nehru later recalled that 'there was no great gulf between him and the Labour leaders at that time'.[2] He took Krishna Menon with him to Cripps's country house, where he found gathered, besides Attlee, Aneurin Bevan, Richard Crossman, Leonard Barnes, and Harold Laski. The party discussed the means by which the next Labour government would transfer power. A constituent assembly would be set up on the basis of universal suffrage, subject to separate minority representation and the election of members from states whose princes accepted the procedure. Once the constitution was passed the Crown's treaties with the princes would lapse. However, the free Indian government would be required to enter into a set-term treaty with Britain, providing for the discharge of Britain's obligations and the protection of its interests during a transitional period.

In London a fortnight later Nehru told a meeting that all-India federation must be scrapped in favour of a constituent assembly.[3] He was speaking to the India Conciliation Group, which, at Gandhi's behest, had been set up in 1931 to promote 'mutual understanding between Great Britain and India'.[4] It

[1] C. R. Attlee, 'As It Happened', MS. in Attlee Papers, Churchill College, Cambridge, ATLE 1/13. See also L. Barnes, Empire and Democracy (1939), 265–7; P. S. Gupta, Imperialism and the British Labour Movement, 1914–1964 (1975), 257–9.

[2] R. G. Coupland, Diary: India, 1941–1942 (hereafter C.D.), 29 Jan. 1942, Coupland Papers, Rhodes House, Oxford.

[3] Notes on meetings of India Conciliation Group (hereafter I.C.G. Notes), subcommittee meeting with Nehru, 14 July 1938, Friends' House, London.

[4] Irene Harrison, Agatha Harrison: An Impression of Her Sister (1956). For a general account of the I.C.G., see H. R. Tinker, 'The India Conciliation Group, 1931–1950: Dilemmas of the Mediator', Journal of Commonwealth and Comparative Politics, XIV (Nov. 1976), 224–41.

consisted largely of Quakers, among them Carl Heath, Horace Alexander, and Alexander Wilson, though its energetic honorary secretary, Agatha Harrison, did not become a Quaker until 1940.[1] At Friends' House in September Nehru insisted that the 'first step to be conceded is the acceptance of the right of India to determine her own constitution'.[2]

In the month following the Munich crisis Nehru felt that the gulf between the policies of Congress and the Raj might be more readily bridged in 'a state of flux': 'it might not be difficult for Congress to state its position in the setting of a larger conflict—and to try to do this by the method of conciliation'.[3] Congress and Britain might agree upon freedom as the object of an anti-Fascist war; for the prize of post-war freedom India might well support the allied cause. Nehru recalled years later that on the eve of the war Indian resentment at the delay of independence might have been transformed by 'a pleasant shock'.[4]

Ten days after the declaration of war, on 14 September 1939, the fifteen-member executive of the Congress, the Working Committee, called for a statement of British 'war aims . . . in regard to democracy and imperialism', and of how they would 'apply to India and . . . be given effect to in the present'.[5] Congress wanted the right of Indians to frame their own constitution through a constituent assembly and to participate in the war effort through representation in the Viceroy's executive. Nehru saw this as a modest demand for the acknowledgement of India's right to freedom and as a prerequisite to co-operation during the war.[6] Agatha Harrison emphasized to Zetland the moderation of Congress leaders, pleading for a British response that promised Dominion status after the war and foreshadowed a constituent assembly.

It was in the context of the early wartime verbal skirmishes between Congress and the unyielding Conservative policy-

[1] It is noteworthy that Cripps's stepmother, Marian Parmoor, was a Quaker (see *The Friend*, 11 July 1952), and a member of the I.C.G.
[2] I.C.G. Notes, 3 Sept. 1938.
[3] Ibid. 19 Oct. 1938.
[4] C.D., 29 Jan. 1942.
[5] Resolution of the C.W.C. on the war crisis, 14 Sept. 1939, M. Gwyer and A. Appadorai (eds.), *Speeches and Documents on the Indian Constitution 1921–47*, 2 vols. (1957), ii. 484–8.
[6] C.D., 29 Jan. 1942.

makers that Cripps entered the Indian lists in earnest. He was
aptly described once as 'the Nehru of England'.[1] Both he and
Nehru were born in 1889 of well-to-do lawyer-cum-politician
fathers; both were educated at famous public schools and
Oxbridge, became barrister–politicians, and flirted with
communism in the 1930s. Both seemed born to govern, con-
triving to assume a patrician status while seeming by their
abstemiousness to renounce its fruits.

Until the time of the Congress provincial electoral triumph
Cripps showed little interest in Indian politics. In 1929 it fell to
his father, Lord Parmoor, to defend Labour's support for
Irwin's Dominion status declaration against an attack from
Lord Reading. In 1932 Cripps was briefed to advise the
Nizam of Hyderabad on the implications for his sovereignty of
accession to the proposed federation. His opinion that under
federation the Viceroy would be obliged to accept the advice of
his ministers chilled the Nizam, who had hoped that his
treaty with the Crown would insulate him against interference by the federal authorities in his dominions. Cripps
hailed the Congress victory of 1937 as the achievement of a
national mandate. *Tribune*, the socialist weekly founded with
his financial support at that time, consistently adopted a pro-
Congress, anti-imperialist line. In 1938 he became increasingly
preoccupied with rearmament, while in January 1939 he was
expelled from the Labour Party for seeking a Lab-Lib Popular
Front in order to defeat appeasement. With the outbreak of
war he gave up his highly lucrative Bar practice to devote
himself to public affairs.

On 28 September 1939 Cripps visited the Foreign Secretary,
Lord Halifax, the former Viceroy (as Lord Irwin), to discuss a
private visit that he proposed to make to China and the
U.S.S.R. Both countries were, of course, then beyond the
perimeter of the war, but they were, like India, of immense
potential relevance to it. When the conversation turned to
India Halifax inferred from Cripps's argument that Nehru was
'not so unreasonable as might appear from some other sources',
and he arranged for him to see Zetland.[2] Next day Cripps

---

[1] Diary kept by Cripps and Geoffrey Wilson, 1939–40 (hereafter C.-W.D.),
14 Dec. 1939, copy in possession of Mr. Maurice Shock, Leicester University.
[2] Halifax to Zetland, 28 Sept. 1939, L/PO/258, India Office Library.

urged Zetland to undertake a reconstruction of the British
Indian central assembly so as to reflect the current disposition
of political power in the provinces, and to appoint selected
members of the new body to the Viceroy's executive. The
lapse of the federation scheme for want of sufficient princely
accessions had left the central government of British India
operating under the constitution of 1919, a glaring anachronism
in the existing circumstances. The Cabinet was still considering
its reply to the Congress demand for a statement of policy.

On 3 October in the House of Commons Attlee attacked the
Viceroy, Lord Linlithgow, for his lack of tact in not seeking to
bring India into the war 'on a level with us'. He called for 'a
more imaginative insight in dealing with the Indian people'
and favoured a statement of the sort demanded by Congress.
Zetland was soon faced with a deputation from the opposition
parties seeking a debate in both Houses and an official statement going as far as possible to meet Congress's claims to be
regarded as a willing and equal partner in the war.

When he wrote to Nehru a week later Cripps was not unhope-
ful of a liberal response to the Working Committee's manifesto.
The Labour Party was 'taking up a very good and helpful
attitude and . . . bringing pressure to bear on the Government.'[1]
He expected an early Commons debate. He advised Nehru
against accepting anything short of 'action which proves con-
clusively the faith behind words'. Congress should 'stand as firm
as a rock upon its demands'. His hopes were dashed by Linlithgow's statement on 18 October, which merely reiterated
Britain's commitment to eventual Dominion status, intimated
that after the war Britain would consult Indians about the
modification of the 1935 Act, and offered Indians membership
of an advisory war committee. On 22 October Congress
rejected this 'unequivocal reiteration of the old imperialist
policy' and called for the resignation of its provincial ministries.[2]
Next day Cripps protested to Halifax against the insulting
deficiencies of the policy.

In the Commons' India debate on 26 October Cripps condemned the government's 'lack of appreciation of the new

---

[1] Cripps to Nehru, 11 Oct. 1939, J. Nehru (ed.), *Bunch of Old Letters* (Bombay, 1958).

[2] C.W.C. Resolution, 22 Oct. 1939, *Indian Annual Register*, 1939, ii. 237–9.

circumstances which have inevitably arisen with the coming of the struggle in Europe'. Britain's war aims made India 'a test question in the eyes of the world'. Britain should assure India that its object was self-government after the war; abandon the scheme for federation; provide at once for the election of a new and representative central legislature; ask the majority parties in the new body to form a government and appoint it as the Viceroy's executive: 'On the basis of that immediate rearrangement, and on the basis of our pledge to grant full self-government after the war, we could, I believe, with safety and confidence, invite the whole-hearted cooperation of the Indian people in our effort to establish democracy and freedom in the world.'

Early in November dissatisfaction with official policy among some members from each of the three British parties led Cripps to include India in his forthcoming foreign tour. As the Congress ministries proffered their resignations the widening gulf between government and people gave rise to alarm. Pressure groups and prominent individuals favoured the dispatch of a non-official parliamentary delegation to investigate Congress demands and keep communication open. Among them were the India Conciliation Group, the India League, Halifax, Lord Snell (Labour leader in the House of Lords), the Conservative R. A. Butler (Under-Secretary of State for India, 1932–7), Wedgwood Benn (a former Labour Secretary of State for India), Sir George Schuster (Finance Member of the Viceroy's executive, 1928–34), Sir Stanley Reed (a Unionist M.P.), and even Zetland himself. Cripps's initiative pre-empted this ground.

Nehru welcomed the news of Cripps's intended visit, and Cripps wrote in good heart on 16 November:

The Cabinet at present is unchangeable in its attitude though some of them (Hoare and Halifax) are very anxious for some peaceful solution. I believe that if Linlithgow could be persuaded to make some recommendation as to a solution along the lines of a true constituent assembly within 12 months of the cessation of hostilities with a treaty between that assembly and this country to arrange the handing over over a period of years, there is just a vague possibility that an arrangement might be come to.[1]

---

[1] Cripps to Nehru, 16 Nov. 1939, Jawaharlal Nehru Collection, Nehru Memorial Library, New Delhi.

The hope was not groundless. Cripps's expression of his ideas at a dinner arranged by Schuster made a considerable impact.[1] Halifax, too, was said to have been 'somewhat impressed by conversation' with him, while Zetland became increasingly drawn to the ideas of a constituent assembly and India acquiring Dominion status by means of a treaty.[2] At the behest of Schuster and Butler (the latter stressing that the unity of India was at stake) Sir Findlater Stewart, Permanent Under-Secretary for India, twice discussed with him the constituent assembly and treaty scheme, which was essentially an elaboration of the ideas discussed at Filkins in June 1938.[3]

The heads of a scheme that Cripps sent to Stewart on 24 November opened with a provision that Britain was now willing to grant India Dominion status: 'By that expression is meant, as was made clear by Lord Balfour in 1926, complete self-government and absolute liberty to terminate partnership in the British Commonwealth of Nations.'[4] This decision to implement forthwith Britain's promises of Dominion status conceded the right of Indians to frame their own constitution through a constituent assembly. As an Act of Parliament was necessary to set up the assembly some delay was unavoidable, but the government would bind itself to introduce a bill 'immediately the war is over, or before that time if opportunity occurs'. Cripps envisaged an assembly of some 2,000 members, chosen on the basis of the existing provincial electorates and with the proportional representation of the states' peoples. But he was prepared to accept any alternative assembly agreeable to the Indian parties. Britain would endorse decisions taken by the assembly on a three-fifths vote, provided only that the assembly agreed to enter into a fixed term treaty (he suggested fifteen years) whereby Britain could discharge its obligations to the princes, the minorities, and the services, and for defence, finance, and commerce. Consistently with its avowed purpose, Britain would immediately 'do its utmost in association with the representatives of the Indian people to arrange such expedients as are possible under the existing constitution to

[1] Stewart to Sir Gilbert Laithwaite, 13 Jan. 1940, L/PO/258.
[2] Zetland to Linlithgow, 22 Nov. 1939, Z.C.
[3] Butler to Stewart, 17 Nov. 1939, and Stewart to Laithwaite, 13 Jan. 1940, L/PO/258.
[4] Cripps to Stewart, 24 Nov. 1939, L/PO/252/16, and enclosure.

give the Indian people a larger measure of self-government during the war'.

Though Cripps went to India with a scheme that had attracted some support he had no accreditation whatever. Zetland remained non-committal when, two days before his departure, Cripps sounded him out on how the government would regard his proposals.[1] Stewart refused to offer his blessing.[2] In India Cripps showed his scheme only to Gandhi and Nehru. The visit was essentially a voyage of discovery. As he was to tell his first interlocutors he had gone 'to learn and not to teach anyone anything'.[3]

(iii) The Globetrotter

Cripps took leave of his wife and daughter at his Grosvenor House flat on 30 November. He was accompanied by an Oxford friend of his son's, Geoffrey Wilson, a young barrister and coincidentally a Quaker, whose father was a member of the India Conciliation Group. Between their arrival at Karachi on 7 December and their departure from Calcutta on Boxing Day the travellers visited Allahabad, Delhi, Lahore, Baroda, Hyderabad, Bombay and Wardha. Their days were spent mostly in discussions with officials, political leaders, and journalists, their nights chiefly in trains.

Upon their arrival at Allahabad on 8 December Cripps and Wilson were welcomed by some fifteen Congressmen and garlanded. They stayed two nights with Nehru at his house, Anand Bhawan, which Nehru's father had built beside the

---

[1] Zetland to Linlithgow, 29 Nov. 1939, Z.C.

[2] The point requires emphasis because Cripps left the impression in some quarters that Stewart viewed the scheme with favour. Before Cripps's visit Stewart felt that 'however mischievous he might be, he was scrupulously straight'. Afterwards he complained to Laithwaite, Linlithgow's secretary, that 'at best he has been guilty of wishful thinking to the point of crookedness'. See Laithwaite's note of a conversation with Cripps, 24 Dec. 1939, L/PO/252/16; Stewart to Laithwaite, 13 Jan. 1940, L/PO/258. Yet Cripps told Nehru that though his scheme enjoyed a favourable response in England no one had committed himself to it (Nehru to M. Desai, 9 Dec. 1939, Nehru, *Old Letters*). Cf. the allegations of the viceregal circle that Cripps was guilty of 'crookedness' in his negotiations during the 1942 mission (R. J. Moore, 'The Mystery of the Cripps Mission', *Journal of Commonwealth Political Studies*, XI (1973), 195–211). Cripps's alleged 'crookedness' can be more convincingly represented as over-confidence in the supremacy of his own views than as machiavellian calculation.

[3] C.-W.D., 7 Dec. 1939.

ancestral house that he gave to Congress. Cripps showed Nehru
his scheme and gave him a copy to send on to Gandhi. They
discussed it both at the beginning and the end of his stay. From
his first reaction Nehru seemed to regard it as providing 'some
sort of basis', though he insisted on the need for adult suffrage.[1]
Under the existing provincial franchise the Muslim representatives in the constituent assembly would never agree with
Congress on a constitution for they had class as well as
community interests to protect. Only by undercutting the
Muslim landlords and middle classes through full adult franchise could leaders representative of the Muslim masses be
brought into the assembly. Given adult franchise Congress was
willing to allow special communal representation for the
minorities. After forty-eight hours' reflection Nehru confirmed
that Cripps's scheme was 'broadly . . . on the right lines'.[2] He
did object to the words 'Dominion status', which Indians
mistrusted, and doubted the need for the treaty period to be as
long as fifteen years and for it to provide for minority rights,
though he was prepared to protect them in the constitution.
Reporting to Mahadev Desai, Gandhi's secretary, he remarked
that the scheme had some desirable features but also had 'two
or three fatal defects'.[3]

On Sunday 10 December Cripps and Wilson boarded their
first Indian train. They spent the Monday in Delhi. From interviews with G. D. Birla, the industrialist supporter of Congress
at whose house the Working Committee was to meet during
the 1942 mission, and Liaquat Ali Khan, Cripps began to glean
the complexities of the communal problem. Birla admitted
that Congress may have been seriously at fault in excluding
non-Congress Muslims from provincial cabinets in 1937. In
consequence talented Muslims, such a Liaquat in Uttar
Pradesh, felt themselves consigned to permanent opposition.
Now they wanted not merely cultural safeguards but an
equal voice in politics, with power to veto legislation inimical
to them. Congress would not entertain such a dereliction of
democratic responsible government. Birla saw only one solution: separate Hindu and Muslim nations, with the cession of

[1] Ibid. 8 Dec. 1939.
[2] Ibid. 10 Dec. 1939.
[3] Nehru to Desai, 9 Dec. 1939, loc. cit.

districts and appropriate population movements, followed, perhaps, by a loose federation holding the minimum powers necessary.

Liaquat corroborated Birla's gloomy analysis. The time for safeguards was passed. The Muslims now wanted a settlement of the communal question on constitutional lines prior to the settlement of the imperial issue. The experience of Congress provincial government had convinced Muslims that western democracy was unsuitable to India. It was necessary to find a constitution that rendered government by the majority community impossible without a defined measure of minority support. Liaquat sketched three possible constitutional solutions: partition; free sovereign states, with Hindu and Muslim federations, and a confederation; and Dominion status for each province, with a federal government exercising such powers as they chose to cede, subject to their right to opt out.[1] The implication of the Muslim position for Cripps's scheme was that the League would not attend a constituent assembly free to devise a constitution by a three-fifths majority vote.

On 11 December Cripps took the overnight train for Lahore pondering a new thought:

There emerges a picture of a rather loose federation of provinces with few reserved subjects and with the right of the provinces to withdraw if they wish and new boundaries to make provinces either predominantly Muslim or Hindu—as the sort of lines of a possible settlement, with a constituent assembly to work out the scheme. It might be necessary to agree the basis of the outcome of the constituent assembly in advance.[2]

Cripps and Wilson spent Tuesday 12 December at Lahore, capital of the Punjab, which was governed by a Unionist, essentially Muslim, ministry. Discussions with the Premier, Sikander Hyat Khan, corroborated the trend of Cripps's thoughts of a settlement in terms of a loose federation as a prior condition of detailed constitution-making.

Cripps met Jinnah at his house on Malabar Hill, Bombay, on Friday 15 December. Jinnah underlined the impossibility

---

[1] C.-W.D., 11 Dec. 1939. Remarkably, Liaquat's three solutions correspond broadly to the three major British answers to the Indian problem in the 1940s: Cripps's 'local option' (1942), the Cabinet Mission's three-tier scheme (1946), and Mountbatten's partition (1947).

[2] Ibid.

of western democracy in India, with its inevitable permanent entrenchment of the majority community. He instanced acts of petty tyranny committed in the Congress provinces after 1937. While some of them, like the adoption of the Hindu flag and anthem, were largely symbolic, others revealed a will to dominate and exclude all but Congressmen from office. He confirmed that 'a Constituent Assembly was not the correct procedure until you had kicked out Great Britain', that 'the power factor had to be decided first'.[1] His immediate proposals were 'that Congress should accept the Muslim League as the negotiator on behalf of the Muslims, that Muslims should be represented in the provincial governments and that no bill should be proceeded with if two-thirds of the Muslim members of the legislature objected to it on communal grounds'. Cripps tackled Jinnah on his recent call for Muslims to celebrate 22 December as a 'day of deliverance' from the Congress provincial governments. He felt that Jinnah was quite willing to meet Nehru.

The difficulty of making progress was apparent the next day, when Cripps suggested to Nehru that he should meet Jinnah. Nehru insisted upon the prior cancellation of the deliverance celebrations. It was clear to Cripps that 'Congress are anxious not to do anything to build up Jinnah's power'.[2] Meetings with him seemed to signify the concession of his demand to be regarded as the spokesman of the Muslims.

Cripps spent 19–20 December at Wardha, talking with Gandhi and members of the Working Committee. He saw Gandhi alone with his secretary. Gandhi had 'some verbal criticisms as to "Dominion Status" and one or two other matters' but said that otherwise Cripps's scheme 'would form an acceptable basis for negotiation and arrangement so far as he was concerned'. He was 'quite convinced that the next step must be with the British Government'.[3]

In his last meeting with the Congress leaders, Nehru and Azad, Cripps tried to rephrase his scheme to take account of the objections that had emerged in the course of his tour:

... I put the possibility ... of an offer by G.B. for freedom and a C.A. of some sort, with a resumption by Congress of the governments and the giving of some seats in the governments to the M.L. during

[1] Ibid. 15 Dec. 1939.   [2] Ibid. 16 Dec. 1939.   [3] Ibid. 20 Dec. 1939.

the period up to the C.A. with some representative centre, leaving
the form etc. of the C.A. to be subsequently decided. They thought
the sharing of power could not be made a condition as it would
then only lead to fresh demands but they thought Congress would
be prepared to offer the share of government if the other were
stated and it might be made a part of private negotiations. They
took the view that it was impossible and indeed inadvisable to
negotiate with the M.L. or other minorities in the existing situation
and that any such action would only lead to an accentuation of the
minority demands. . . . The position is therefore that there will be no
direct negotiations and that unless G.B. takes some step which helps
to eliminate the nationalist issue, the M.L. control will continue the
communal agitation.[1]

Throughout his visit Cripps found a general conviction
among British officials and journalists that India would
achieve Dominion status after the war. On 12 December *The
Times* correspondent, Alexander Inglis, 'like everybody else
that I have seen, took dominion status for granted within the
quite near future at the end of the war'.[2] Lumley, Governor of
Bombay, seemed 'perfectly prepared for the granting of
Dominion status immediately after the war.'[3] Haig, recently
Governor of Uttar Pradesh, thought there was a 'lack of co-
ordination between British opinion and that in British India'.[4]
There had been 'a great advance in the views of Anglo-
Indians, especially in the first days of the war. . . . A generous
statement made with conviction at that time could have
settled the troubles.' Even Sir Reginald Maxwell, the reputedly
diehard Home Member of the Government of India, 'seemed
to take for granted a free India in the near future'.[5]

Neither was there much sympathy in British India for the
extension of paramountcy to protect the princes once Dominion
status was established. Cripps had no discussions with the
Political Department, but he did have a memorable meeting
with the Nizam of Hyderabad, the largest of the states:

I pointed out that freedom would almost certainly be given to
British India after the war. . . . Paramountcy would then have to
disappear of necessity since there would be no troops in British India
and presumably the states would not wish to have British troops

---

[1] Ibid.   [2] Ibid. 12 Dec. 1939.   [3] Ibid. 15 Dec. 1939.
[4] Ibid. 16 Dec. 1939.   [5] Ibid. 12 Dec. 1939.

permanently stationed in them and he accepted the proposition. I then suggested that such a situation would be covered by the British Government giving notice to terminate paramountcy after the period of a short term treaty with British India and that that period should be used by the states for arguing the basis of federation with British India. He seemed to consider this a feasible proposal.[1]

The Nizam's Diwan, Sir Akbar Hydari, agreed with Cripps's propositions on paramountcy. He visualized 'the British question being first settled, when negotiations between the British Indian parties and the states could take place'.

Cripps did not refine the vaguely phrased passage in his scheme that envisaged the association of party representatives with the central government during the war. In his Commons speech of 26 October he had been specific about the election of a central legislature by the existing provincial legislatures and an invitation from the Viceroy to the majority parties to act as his executive:

It is true that, technically and in accordance with the constitution, the Executive Council would not be a Cabinet, but there is no reason on earth why our Government should not give an undertaking that the Viceroy would deal with the Executive Council . . . as if it were a Cabinet on all major matters; that is to say he would accept their advice as the Crown here accepts the advice of the Cabinet when duly tendered to it.

The fact that such precise terms were not reproduced in the draft scheme of 24 November may reflect the influence of the India experts with whom Cripps spoke in the interval. In any event, it is notable that in his last interview with Nehru and Azad on 20 December he spoke merely of 'some representative centre'. Early in the tour Cripps had formed the impression that Congress was 'more concerned with the ultimate solution of the problem than with any immediate steps that might be taken in the intermediate period',[2] which may have led him to concentrate upon the eventual terms of settlement.

The tour heightened Cripps's awareness of the urgency of the Indian problem. In an early interview at Allahabad he received the impression, subsequently confirmed, that while Congress was prepared to hold its hand for a limited period of

[1] Ibid. 18 Dec. 1939.　　　　[2] Ibid. 9 Dec. 1939.

time in the hope of a solution being arrived at it would not
wait indefinitely for Britain to grant the substance of its re-
quests.[1] The resignation of the Congress ministries made likely
an extra-constitutional campaign to strengthen the Congress
mandate. At the same time, Jinnah's appeal for a day of deliverance warned of the danger that communal feeling would
be exacerbated by direct action.

Cripps's general conclusion was that the Muslim League's
opposition to democratic constitution-making rendered insufficient a simple promise of post-war Dominion status accompanied by the offer of a constituent assembly and a treaty. The
League required guarantees of the Muslims' political integrity
—some constitutional scheme to secure them against the
emergence of Hindu raj—before they would join in making a
constitution. Prior negotiations between the League and Congress were therefore vital. Yet Congress shrank from taking an
initiative that seemed to recognize the authority of the League
to negotiate for the Muslims. Britain must intervene to offer a
constitutional prospect acceptable to both parties, as a prerequisite to their co-operation.

Again and again Cripps's informants told him that only the
Viceroy could bring the two sides together. On 13 December,
after a day in Delhi with officials, politicans, and journalists,
Cripps noted: 'The general impression that I gained from
today's interviews, superimposed on what had gone before, was
that the deadlock would only be broken if the Viceroy started
real negotiations on the basis of a firm British offer in generous
terms and that unless this were done soon, there was extreme
danger of the most serious situation arising.'[2] Equally, Cripps
concluded that among Indians and Englishmen alike there
were serious doubts about the Viceroy's negotiating skills. On
18 December, before he had met Linlithgow, he noted:

I told Hydari of my suspicions that the Viceroy was not by nature a
negotiator at all but rather a judge and he confirmed this and like
other people have [sic] told me that one of the difficulties was that
the Viceroy never disclosed what was in his mind so that it was
impossible to know how far if at all arguments addressed to him had
been fully appreciated. Everyone stresses his sincerity and good will
but suggests that he is the wrong man for the particular job in hand.[3]

[1] Ibid.   [2] Ibid. 13 Dec. 1939.   [3] Ibid. 8 Dec. 1939.

Cripps's last stop before his departure for Rangoon on 26 December was at Calcutta where, in observance of the almanac of viceregal visitations, Linlithgow was staying. Cripps discussed his scheme with both Linlithgow and his secretary, Sir Gilbert Laithwaite. He urged the Viceroy to bring the parties together to discuss a settlement:

I told him that, in my view, negotiations between the Moslem League and the Congress were out of the question at present unless a third party brought them together and that *he* was the only possible third party; also that they should be asked to put down in writing, Congress, how far it was prepared to go in meeting the Moslem demands, and the Moslem League, exactly what demands it made, so that he might compare the two statements and attempt to bridge the difference by negotiation. . . . I further told him that in my view, unfortunately, Zetland had little power or authority in England, and that owing to the preoccupation of other members of the Cabinet with war questions he, as Viceroy, was in fact the most important determining factor on the question of Indian policy. . . . I left him with a copy of the memorandum which I prepared in London and told him of Gandhi's reaction to it.[1]

He reported to Nehru:

On the whole I am not at all displeased, though the rather sphinx-like nature of the Viceroy made it difficult to find what is cooking in his mind. . . . I am sure he wants sincerely to settle the matter if he can. I don't think there is any question of his playing the Moslems against the Hindus—that stage has passed. I told him my view of Zetland and the British Government and therefore the need for him to initiate the right policy from this end.[2]

In fact, during Cripps's absence, Zetland had initiated a policy not unlike Cripps's own scheme.

To follow Linlithgow's response to Cripps it is necessary to take up the question in the dialogue between the Viceroy and his masters in London.

[1] Quoted in E. Estorick, *Stafford Cripps: A Biography* (1949), 206.
[2] Cripps to Nehru, 24 Dec. 1939, J.N. Coll.

THE FIRST OFFER
(September 1939–September 1941)

(i) The Test of War

WHEN WAR broke out Britain had no constitutional policy for
India. On 1 September, when the extended term for the accession of the princes expired, only a quarter of them had signed
instruments. Since his assumption of office in 1936 Linlithgow
had striven hard to bring the federation to life. In his willingness to bargain with the princes over the terms of their accession
he had been well ahead of the Cabinet, which, even in August
1939 when the failure of their policy was certain, favoured a
waiting game. Zetland had even shied away from his suggestion that a parliamentary declaration should be made of
Britain's policy to introduce a federation as soon as possible. A
declaration would provoke Churchill and the diehards, whose
reaction would only encourage princely intransigence. On 11
September Linlithgow suspended negotiations for establishing
the federation. He had the concurrence of Zetland, who did
not even need to bring the matter before the Cabinet.

Though clearly impracticable, the policy of federation was
shelved rather than abandoned; for neither the Viceroy nor the
Cabinet was prepared to face the constitutional implications of
the importance of Congress. Linlithgow committed India to the
war without consulting the party that then governed eight of the
eleven provinces. When Congress appealed for a clarification
of Britain's war aims in relation to India, he noted: 'It is a
tragedy in many ways that at a time such as this we should
have in so important a position a doctrinaire like Nehru, with
his amateur knowledge of foreign politics and of the inter-

national stage.'[1] At the beginning of October he interviewed
Gandhi, Nehru, Rajendra Prasad (then Congress president),
and Jinnah. Though disappointed at the tenor of the discussion
Nehru followed up with a desperate letter of personal entreaty
that exposed the shallowness of Linlithgow's judgement:

I want . . . to tell you how much I desire that the long conflict of
India and England should be ended and that they should cooperate
together. I have felt that this war, with all its horrors, has brought
this opportunity to our respective countries and it would be sad and
tragic if we are unable to take advantage of it. . . . May I say how
much I appreciate your friendly courtesy to me? It was a pleasure
to meet you for a second time, and whenever chance offers an
opportunity for this again, I shall avail myself of it.[2]

They never met again.

Linlithgow sent home his proposals for a reply to Congress: a
statement that Britain's object was Dominion status; that after
the war the government, in conjunction with Indian leaders,
would reconsider the federal scheme; and that immediately
non-officials would be 'associated in a consultative capacity
with the Central Government of India with a view to receiving
information and tendering advice as to the conduct of affairs
in India in relation to the war'.[3] At its first discussion on the
proposal the Cabinet was critical, fearing the entrenchment of
the advisory committee in the machinery of government. It
sought details of the proposed committee's composition and
functions, and an assurance that the members would be invited
to attend particular meetings for particular purposes and not as
of right. Linlithgow gave such an assurance, adding that communal differences and the avoidance of voting would mini-
mize the risk to the Viceroy's authority. On 14 October the
Cabinet approved the text of Linlithgow's statement but
limited the declaration of Britain's object to the achievement by
India of its 'due place amongst the Dominions'.[4] The statement
appeared on 18 October.

It was no surprise to Linlithgow when Congress rejected his

[1] Linlithgow to Zetland, 18 Sept. 1939, Z.C.
[2] Nehru to Linlithgow, 6 Oct. 1939, quoted in S. Gopal, *Jawaharlal Nehru: A Biography*, I (1975), 255.
[3] Memo. by Zetland, 'India and the War', 25 Sept. 1939, for War Cabinet on 27 Sept. 1939, Conclusion 29 (39) 12, Public Record Office (P.R.O.).
[4] Cabinet Conclusion 47 (39) 12, 14 Oct. 1939.

statement and repeated its demands for a share in the central
government during the war and a post-war constituent assembly.
However, he was clearly dismayed that Congress backed its
stand with an appeal to its provincial ministries to resign. He
consoled himself that neither he nor Zetland nor the Cabinet
should 'feel that there is anything which we have left undone
which we ought to have done or that we have spared any
effort to reach a reasonable accommodation'.[1] Yet he had
certainly underestimated the gravity of the situation, misread-
ing the sincerity and resolution behind the war aims manifesto.
Under pressure he was now prepared to improve his offer.
Whereas in September he had decided that there was 'no
prospect whatever . . . of creating a temporary or war centre',[2]
he now sought Cabinet approval for further meetings with the
Indian leaders to seek an agreed basis whereby they would
accept seats on an enlarged central executive. At that stage, the
Viceroy's executive was still composed, pursuant to the provisions of the 1919 India Act, of the Viceroy, the Commander-
in-Chief, three British officials with ten years' experience of
India, and three non-official Indians.

Zetland commended the advance to the Cabinet on 25
October.

I told the Cabinet very plainly that while we had supposed that the
journey towards Dominion Status would be a long one, the effect
of the outbreak of war had been to bring us hard up against the
implications of Dominion Status for India and I told them that they
must make up their minds how far they were now prepared to go
to implement the promises contained in our earlier pledges. I
pointed out that we were on the horns of a painful dilemma: that
there were two courses open to us, each of which was attended by
considerable disadvantages. One was to take our stand on your
statement with the practical certainty that this would mean fighting
Congress and taking over the government in eight Congress provinces. The other possible course was to consider what further
steps could immediately be taken to meet the claims of the Congress
in the hope of finding a compromise which would be regarded by the
Right Wing as sufficiently attractive to justify them in co-operating
with us.[3]

[1] Linlithgow to Zetland, 22 Oct. 1939, Z.C.
[2] Linlithgow to Zetland, 26 Sept. 1939, Z.C.
[3] Zetland to Linlithgow, 26 Oct. 1939, Z.C.

Chamberlain's Cabinet contained the leaders of the appeasers, Sir Samuel Hoare (Lord Privy Seal), Sir John Simon (Chancellor of the Exchequer), and Lord Halifax (Foreign Secretary). They were also the men whom Churchill, now First Lord of the Admiralty, had despised as 'pygmies' responsible for Britain's India policy. As Viceroy (1926–31), Halifax had initiated the Round Table Conference approach to constitution-making, the declaration of Britain's intention to make India a Dominion, and the truce with Gandhi that ended the civil disobedience movement of 1929–31. Simon, the head of the Indian Statutory Commission, had at first thought India unready for central responsibility but had accepted the federation scheme as consistent with the principles of his report. Hoare, as Secretary of State (1931–5), was the chief architect of the India Act and did more than anyone to secure the Conservative Party's support for it.

In the Cabinet discussion of Linlithgow's proposed move Churchill was adamant against 'yielding to the pressures of parties who were, after all, only exploiting the dangers with which Britain was faced'.[1] The Cabinet should avoid the 'slippery slope' of accepting whatever the Indian parties agreed upon, and assure the Viceroy that it would 'stand by him in a policy of firm administration' if the Congress ministries resigned. Simon, too, felt that concessions would only stimulate further demands. However, the Cabinet was impressed by the grave prospect of a non-co-operation movement in wartime. Sir John Anderson, a former Governor of Bengal (1932–7), now Home Secretary, favoured giving Indians further experience of government by transferring portfolios to them, while Halifax went so far as to propose a reconstruction of the central government that could be presented as a 'National Indian War Cabinet'. The first meeting on the matter adjourned without reaching a conclusion. At a second meeting the same day Chamberlain came out in support of Linlithgow's move. The Cabinet agreed, subject to the Viceroy being instructed that in any change three tests must be satisfied: the supreme power of the Viceroy must remain intact; Britain's freedom to deploy forces in India must not be affected; there must be no constitutional legislation during the war and no promises that

[1] Cabinet Conclusion, 59 (39) 8, 25 Oct. 1939.

would bind Parliament after the war. The tests were Churchill's.[1]

A few days later Linlithgow sounded out Gandhi, Prasad, and Jinnah on the possibility of Congress and the League agreeing the basis on which they would accept seats on an enlarged executive. It became clear that Congress would not enter the executive without a prior declaration of India's right to frame its own independent constitution after the war. On the other hand, Jinnah would not agree to such a declaration until Congress had recognized the League as the voice of India's Muslims and redressed its grievances, including its exclusion from the ministries in Congress provinces. Early in October Linlithgow had already concluded that 'there is no basis for agreement between the communities and the political interests with which we are dealing'.[2] In the middle of the month, at the conclusion of a series of meetings with political leaders, he recorded his

far stronger impression than I had previously of the reality of the divergence of view between these various interests and communities. I had not, possibly, fully realized till now how greatly the gap between Hindu and Muslim has widened since April 1937, or the extent to which experiences, whether real or imaginary, . . . since then have undermined altogether belief in the possibility of common and united action on which the Act of 1935 was so essentially based.[3]

He ought therefore to have expected his initiative at the end of the month to fail, for it made the reconstruction of his council dependent upon agreement and assumed common action. He would now espouse a policy of inaction.

On 6 November a special Cabinet meeting was unanimous that Britain should not concede India's right to post-war independence and a constituent assembly. Halifax, its most liberal member, was disturbed that by requiring Congress–League agreement as a condition of central reconstruction Britain was exposing itself to the charge of pursuing a deliberate policy of divide and rule. He favoured making every effort to help India to achieve unity. Hoare, too, was anxious. He was prepared to abandon the old waiting game and favoured an early attempt to bring federation into being: the princes, especially the

[1] Cabinet Conclusion, 60 (39) 1, 25 Oct. 1939.
[2] Linlithgow to Zetland, 7 Oct. 1939, Z.C.
[3] Linlithgow to Zetland, 16 Oct. 1939, Z.C.

Nizam, might be pressed, and perhaps they would now co-operate with the Muslims.[1] The Cabinet had already given Linlithgow general approval to proceed with discussions on a federation if opportunity arose, and it now seemed likely to agree a conclusion requiring him to revive the sleeping monster. However, Churchill scotched the proposal, arguing convincingly that a federation had been exposed as unwanted by princes and Congress alike. The Cabinet resolved to support the Vice-roy and the Governors in maintaining law and order as the Congress ministries resigned, but agreed that Congress should not be obstructed in any co-operative overture that it might make.

In the course of November, as the Congress ministries with-drew from office, section ninety-three of the 1935 India Act was applied to seven provinces. It provided that in the event of a breakdown of the constitutional machinery the powers exercised by the ministry would revert to the Governor. This withdrawal of Congress from provincial politics increased the relative importance of the League. Though as yet it was not strong enough to take over in such Congress provinces as Assam (where a coalition was now established), and the Muslim majority N.W.F.P., the League was presented with the even-tual opportunity of doing so. In addition, as a national party of growing importance the League now had greater leverage in the non-Congress provinces of Sind, Bengal, and the Punjab.

Concerned at the reversion to official government, Zetland began to turn towards Cripps's scheme. On 22 November he sounded out Linlithgow: 'Would it be a practicable proposition, I wonder, to say to the Congress: "Very well! Go ahead with your Constituent Assembly and we will ratify the constitution

---

[1] Cabinet Conclusion 73 (39) 1. Like Cripps and Attlee, Hoare saw the implica-tions of the war for Indian policy: 'I feel . . . myself that just as it was impossible to keep constitutional discussions out of the last war, e.g. Montagu and Chelmsford, so it will be impossible to keep them out of this war. In the present case there is this additional factor, that one of our principal war aims seems to be freedom, and freedom in India will be interpreted by many people as meaning responsible Government at the Centre' (Hoare to Zetland, 22 Oct. 1939, L/PO/258). He thought very poorly of Linlithgow's 18 October statement and suggested the need for Linlithgow to be more elastic and less negative on the question of constitutional discussions. However, unlike his Labour adversaries he failed to see the inadequacy of the all-India federation scheme.

which you produce provided that it is accepted voluntarily by
the minorities and the Princes." '[1] Power would be transferred
by a treaty. Linlithgow regarded 'all this talk of Treaties and of
Constituent Assemblies with the utmost misgiving' and urged
the need to avoid being 'bounced' by Congress into arrangements inimical to the Muslims and the princes.[2] Zetland was
not to be put off. On 29 November he argued the advantage of
letting India solve the communal problem through a constituent assembly. He intimated that he would raise the matter
with the Prime Minister.[3]

Zetland told Chamberlain that while the transition to
official government had gone smoothly Congress would not
remain quiescent. In the background was the menace of civil
disobedience. Moreover, it could not be assumed that after
the war Britain could pick up the threads of its policy of
advance by 'smooth, measured and leisurely stages'. War
churned the ocean of thought. 'There are a number of influences
tending at the present time towards a leap forward. The most
recent—which is the immediate cause of this letter—is not at
first sight of great significance, yet is one which may prove to
be of considerable effect. The instrument is Sir Stafford
Cripps.'[4] If Cripps were able to get the Indian leaders to agree
to his plan 'we should find it very difficult on moral grounds
alone to resist it'. Zetland attached importance to the propaganda value of Britain conceding the constituent assembly.
For if the Indians could not agree upon such a procedure, or
upon the assembly's constitution, then the world would see
that not British interests but Indian divisions were responsible
for the political impasse.

Chamberlain did not dissent from the view that the time had
come for a forward move. He was prepared to consider the
Cripps proposal. He agreed therefore that Zetland should write
to Linlithgow to this effect but 'make it clear that this was a
provisional view and subject to anything the Viceroy might
wish to say'.[5] Zetland wrote gleefully to Linlithgow that

[1] Z.C.
[2] Linlithgow to Zetland, 27 Nov. 1939, Z.C.
[3] To Linlithgow, 29 Nov. 1939, Z.C.
[4] Zetland to N. Chamberlain, 1 Dec. 1939, Prem. 1/414.
[5] Minute of meeting between Zetland and P.M., 4 Dec. 1939, ibid.

Neville Chamberlain himself is quite ready to consider favourably what not so long ago would have been regarded as a revolutionary proposal. Whether Cabinet as a whole would be receptive I cannot say. Edward Halifax would be favourably disposed and I think that Sam Hoare would very likely be also. Simon might be rather sticky and Winston Churchill would clearly have to be approached with very great caution.[1]

Zetland enclosed a draft statement by the British government which stressed: 'It is our policy to *promote* by every means in our power the advance of India to the status of a fully self-governing Dominion.'

Linlithgow's immediate reaction on 18 December was 'most definitely (judging the position in the terms of the atmosphere and the attitude of the parties here) that anything on these lines is not only well ahead of necessity but would have the most serious reactions on the whole Indian position'.[2] Like Cripps, Linlithgow had come to realize that the Muslim League would resent any promise of a constituent assembly without the prior settlement of the constitutional problem. Such a declaration would further inflame Muslim opinion, of which Jinnah's call for a day of deliverance was an ominous indication.

On 21 December Linlithgow made a lengthy analysis of the position and sketched an alternative course of action.[3] In order to destroy it, he rehearsed the case for 'a radical and imaginative move': first, it was necessary to restore parliamentary government in the provinces and to secure the goodwill of Congress, the League, and the princes; secondly, the present impasse was a setback for the policy of constitutional advance, offended international and British parliamentary opinion, and impeded the war effort; thirdly, the majority community's demands afforded the best escape from the impasse, subject to the acceptance of a constituent assembly by the minorities and the conclusion of a treaty covering Britain's interests and obligations. Linlithgow disputed that the time had come for so radical an approach. There was little chance of a Hindu–Muslim agreement upon a constituent assembly, and to defer to the Congress demand would only make Congress more unreasonable and

[1] Zetland to Linlithgow, 6 Dec. 1939, Z.C.
[2] Cable to Zetland, Z.C.
[3] Linlithgow to Zetland, Z.C.

antagonize the Muslims (who were still, after all, working within the provincial sections of the 1935 Act). If Britain yielded to Congress now, the party would use its enhanced prestige to drive a hard bargain over Britain's commercial interests. Linlithgow's emphasis was primarily imperialist:

After all we framed the Constitution as it stands in the Act of 1935, because we thought that way the best way—given the political position in both countries—of maintaining British influence in India. It is no part of our policy, I take it, to expedite in India constitutional changes for their own sake, or gratuitously to hurry the handing over of the controls to Indian hands at any pace faster than that which we regard as best calculated, on a long view, to hold India to the Empire.

Linlithgow also questioned whether a treaty period of fifteen years allowed enough time for Britain to feel assured that its obligations to the Muslims and the princes could be transferred. As for a constituent assembly, how could Britain give it *carte blanche* when it might frame a constitution inimical to unity or democracy, or whose safeguards of minority rights might prove illusory? Britain could not ignore the possible need to re-enter the Indian scene in the event of disagreement at the constituent assembly or treaty stage.

Linlithgow proposed to pause a while, and then see Gandhi and Jinnah separately in an attempt to bring them to an agreement over the provinces. If he succeeded, then he would call ten or a dozen Indian leaders together and seek: their ratification of minority safeguards in the provinces as required by Jinnah and accepted by Gandhi; their agreement to a temporary expansion of the Viceroy's executive; their approval for a formal statement that Britain's object was Dominion status or independence within the Empire; and that 'we should by agreement move immediately into Federation as soon as the necessary mechanical processes could be completed . . . with a view to proceeding with the minimum delay through that stage into the Dominion status stage; and if possible before the conclusion of the war'.

Zetland was all for Linlithgow trying something on these lines, though he was pessimistic about the outcome. He was particularly enthusiastic about an exploratory discussion of the problem by a small and competent body of politicians, which, indeed, he had himself suggested as early as May, when he had anticipated that the opposition of the Muslims and the princes would stalemate the federal scheme.[1] It was also, of course, the first step that Cripps was to propose to Linlithgow three days later.

Linlithgow began to put his plan into effect in January during a visit to Bombay. On the 10th, in a speech at the Orient Club, he indicated that Britain's object was Dominion status of the Statute of Westminster variety, and that he would immediately enlarge his executive to include representatives of Congress, the League, and the princes. Gandhi thought he saw some forward movement in the speech and asked to see Linlithgow. A meeting was arranged for 5 February. Meanwhile Linlithgow met Jinnah and ascertained his minimum terms for agreement with Congress: coalition ministries in the provinces; the right of the Muslim members to veto any bill brought before a provincial legislature if two-thirds of them opposed it; the abandonment of the Congress anthem, *Bande Mataram*, and the practice of flying the Congress flag from public buildings.

On 2 February Zetland acquainted the Cabinet of the package by which Linlithgow hoped to secure Gandhi's co-operation: the promise of Dominion status as soon as possible; the enlargement of his executive to include politicians; the inauguration of a federation as soon as the states could be brought in; and subsequent consultation with Indians on the revision of the constitution.[2] Zetland, firmer in his convictions than he had been previously, argued that there was 'no chance of this plan proving the basis of fruitful discussion'. Gandhi would reject it for not fulfilling Congress's demands. The Muslims would require changes in the federal constitution that Congress would oppose. If the talks with Gandhi were not 'to break down almost as soon as they start, the Viceroy must be prepared to offer a closer accommodation to the Congress point of view'. He asked the Cabinet to endorse, as its provisional view, the policy that India should be conceded the right to frame its own post-war Dominion constitution, subject to agreement among

[1] Zetland to Chamberlain, 5 Jan. 1940, Prem. 1/414.
[2] Zetland's Cabinet memo., 31 Jan. 1940 (WP (G) (40) 37); Cabinet 30 (40) 4, 2 Feb. 1940.

the parties on the composition of a constituent assembly and the conclusion of a treaty. Linlithgow should indicate that as a first step towards constitution-making a small conference of Indian leaders would be called. Zetland warned that the result of the failure of Linlithgow's talk with Gandhi could be civil disobedience, which Britain could contain 'only by methods which would expose our general motives in the war to the most effective criticism', not the least in America.

Zetland failed to carry the Cabinet. It merely approved of Linlithgow's discussion with Gandhi. If the approach failed Linlithgow must go no further. In specifying Britain's objectives he must avoid the phrase that he had proposed, 'independence within the Empire', in favour of 'self-governing, or autonomous, communities within the Empire', which was less likely to be construed as implying a right of secession.[1] The opposition to Zetland was led by Churchill and Simon.

Churchill advocated a firm stand against Congress. Since the resumption of official control, 'for the first time for several years the Congress Provinces had been properly administered':

> . . . he did not share the anxiety to encourage and promote unity between the Hindu and Muslim communities. Such unity was, in fact, almost out of the realm of practical politics, while, if it were to be brought about, the immediate result would be that the united communities would join in showing us the door. He regarded the Hindu–Muslim feud as the bulwark of British rule in India.

Simon argued that 'there was every reason for not going any faster than we were obliged to'. Anderson was opposed to offering Congress anything beyond Linlithgow's proposal, and Chamberlain wished to look no further forward for the moment. Only Halifax supported Zetland's view.

The Linlithgow–Gandhi talks were short-lived, despite Linlithgow's assessment that 'if Gandhi is prepared to be reasonable then there is . . . some chance of a settlement' on the Cabinet's approved basis.[2] Gandhi reiterated the claim for a constituent assembly and rejected provincial coalitions. On 6 February Linlithgow advised Zetland that Congress seemed to be gambling that British 'calamities in the field', or 'pressure

---

[1] Ibid.
[2] Linlithgow to Zetland, 3 Feb. 1940, Z.C.

from public opinion at Home', would produce a better offer.[1]
He concluded that there was 'nothing for it now but to lie back
for the present'. A week later he confirmed that it was best to
'refrain from action', to avoid 'running after the Congress'.[2]

Gandhi's abrupt termination of negotiations on 6 February
left Zetland with no opening for referring back to the Cabinet.
He believed that he would have secured some support for a further step, but it was 'possible and perhaps probable' that he
would have met opposition, 'in which case I do not think that
Neville Chamberlain would have been willing to press the
matter to the point of a decision'.[3] However, he felt that the
Cabinet could not object to Linlithgow now calling together a
small conference of political leaders. He seriously underestimated the antagonism of Churchill and Simon, whose confidential approaches to Chamberlain now revealed a hostility
towards even the grudging and limited accommodation that
Linlithgow had offered Congress since the outbreak of war.

On 13 February Simon wrote to Chamberlain at some length
to forestall a fresh approach by Zetland, and because there were
things it was 'difficult to say . . . in Cabinet without seeming to
be unduly critical of others'.[4] He quoted Jinnah's claim that
the Viceroy 'never appeared to break with Gandhi and always
left the impression that he was going to see him before long and
that negotiations would be resumed. This', wrote Simon, 'is a
perfectly well-founded criticism of our handling of Indian
politics for a long time past and it is a course of conduct full
of the gravest danger.' Offering more and more to Congress
produced 'the impression that we are in continuous retreat',
and it could 'only end in our collapse'.

Churchill wrote to Chamberlain that he was entirely in
agreement with Simon: 'The policy of running after Gandhi
and the Congress, which the Viceroy conceives it his duty to
pursue, is steadily wearing down every pillar of British authority.
The Secretary of State ought to send him clear instructions
defining and correcting his course during the war.'[5]

As Linlithgow himself now looked back to the outbreak of war

[1] Letter, Z.C.
[2] Linlithgow to Zetland, 13 Feb. 1940, Z.C.
[3] Zetland to Linlithgow, 28 Feb. 1940, Z.C.
[4] Simon to Chamberlain, 13 Feb. 1940, Prem. 1/414.
[5] Churchill to Chamberlain, 20 Feb. 1940, ibid.

he realized that things had 'advanced at a far more rapid pace than anyone had imagined':

We have agreed in principle to a variety of things to bridge the interim period—the expansion of my Council, first the suspension then the revival of the federal idea during war time; we have further agreed to reopen the scheme and the policy of the Act of 1935 and to consult all concerned on any alternative scheme. Finally we have committed ourselves to Dominion status, though we have also made it clear that we shall look after the legitimate interests of the minorities.[1]

For the moment Linlithgow was resolved 'to lie back and not to move'. Britain had offered all that it practically could. The next move must lie with the Indian parties: 'They must get together themselves and they must reach their own agreement.' He was not opposed in principle to convening a small conference of politicians but was 'not in favour of doing it for some time to come'. He was willing to admit that war had imposed 'a stern and searching test' upon British and Indian plans, which had not emerged 'as we would have wished they might'.

Zetland did try once more, on 15 March, to persuade the Cabinet to adopt his 'constructive plan of action'.[2] However, there was pending a Congress Working Committee resolution calling for complete independence and the framing of a constitution by an assembly based on manhood suffrage. Zetland's memorandum was set aside. On 12 April it was shelved. In the interim Congress, in full session at Ramgarh, had passed the Working Committee's resolution, and the League, meeting at Lahore, had passed the famous Pakistan resolution, calling for the creation of separate and sovereign Muslim nations.

Despite Zetland's efforts, between November 1939 and March 1940 neither the Viceroy nor the Cabinet was prepared to espouse the Crippsian strategy of opening negotiations with representatives of Congress and the League on the basis of India's right to frame its own constitution. It is impossible to know whether a skilful diplomatist could have prevented the resort by the parties to the extreme demands that they expounded at Ramgarh and Lahore. But in retrospect it does seem that the conclusions drawn by Cripps in December 1939 were more

[1] Linlithgow to Zetland, 27 Feb. 1940, Z.C.
[2] Zetland Cabinet memo., 11 Mar. 1940 (WP (G) (40) 73).

consonant with political realities than official British strategy. In March Cripps wrote to Nehru from China, regretting that the British government was behaving 'so stupidly, as I had some hope after my talks with the Viceroy that matters might improve'.[1]

(ii) The August Offer

When Cripps returned to England in April he told Findlater Stewart that he did not believe the Hindus and the Muslims would ever reach agreement in Linlithgow's time. Soon after Churchill formed his government on 10 May, Cripps had a talk with Leopold Amery, the incoming Secretary of State for India, and showed him his scheme. He argued the need to decide whether to coerce or conciliate Congress, for there was danger of civil disobedience. Favouring conciliation, Cripps urged that Britain should announce that India would have the right to settle its own future, and send out a team of two or three negotiators—say, Wedgwood Benn, Sir Malcolm Hailey, and Sir Stanley Reed—to bring the parties together.[2] Reiterating the divergences of Indian opinion only inflamed the situation. It was necessary to find 'a line of agreement and work from that'. This was, for the moment, Cripps's parting shot at the Indian problem. Before the end of the month he was on his way to Moscow, where he was to remain as ambassador until January 1942.

If Cripps's representations were insufficient to persuade Amery to reopen the constitutional question, a further inducement was soon provided by his realization of what the probable alternative, coercion, would mean. Towards the end of May Linlithgow sought Cabinet approval to enact a Revolutionary Movements Ordinance, conferring extraordinary powers in the event of civil disobedience. The Ordinance declared the whole of the Congress organization unlawful. It provided for the arrest of its leaders and the seizure of its bank balances and premises. It gave the Viceroy power to declare the movement revolutionary, whereupon the government could proceed

[1] Cripps to Nehru, 18 Mar. 1940, J.N. Coll.
[2] I.C.G. Notes, 24 May 1940; Cripps to A. Harrison, 20 May 1940, I.C.G. Box 47 (Cripps).

against a wide range of activities not in themselves breaches of the law. On 1 June Amery secured the Cabinet's general approval of the scheme of the Ordinance but subject to the Government of India obtaining its prior consent to the scheme's implementation.

Yet further reason for a fresh constitutional initiative was provided by the dire course of events in Europe. The end of the phoney war and the rapid German advance into Belgium, Holland, and France gave additional cause for not provoking a revolutionary movement and for enlisting full co-operation in India.

On 2 June Amery proposed to Linlithgow that Britain should concede India's right to frame its own constitution, subject to suitable arrangements being made for the discharge of British responsibilities. Provided that the Indian parties could agree upon its form, a constituent assembly should be set up after the war. Linlithgow demurred. The time was not propitious for a further overture. On 17 June Amery urged him most strongly to appeal to Indians to find some agreed basis for entering the provincial and central governments. To this end he would announce that Britain's object was for a united India to become 'a partner–member in the British Commonwealth of Nations on the same footing of Independence as the United Kingdom and the Dominions'.[1] Britain would establish a postwar constituent assembly, given Indian agreement on its form, and would accept any agreed constitution that it produced, subject only to the Indian Dominion signing an Instrument of Agreement with regard to defence, the sterling debt, the services, commerce, and the princely states remaining in the Dominion.

Linlithgow remained unconvinced, but in the aftermath of the fall of France he asked Gandhi to see him. He tested out Gandhi on whether a declaration clarifying the 'intentions of His Majesty's Government, particularly in regard to dates and times', might ease the way for Congress participation in the central and provincial governments.[2] He outlined two main concessions. First:

... as regards main constitutional scheme and framing of future constitution, on assumption that matters just mentioned [i.e. British

[1] Amery to Linlithgow, 17 June 1940, L/PO/6/105d.
[2] Linlithgow to Amery, 1 July 1940 (cable), ibid.

interests and obligations] were protected in some suitable manner
His Majesty's Government would be perfectly content to abide by
conclusions of any representative body of Indians on which various
political parties could agree, and that . . . it might be assumed that
Parliament would implement recommendations of such a body so
long as they were based on agreement.

And second:

. . . at point matters had now reached and in view of obvious mis-
understandings to which their reluctance . . . to fix and proclaim a
time limit or date had given rise, I thought it not impossible that His
Majesty's Government might be found ready to take chance and to
say that . . . they would spare no effort to bring about Dominion
status within a year after conclusion of the war.

Gandhi remained adamant on the full Congress demand for
independence as elaborated at Ramgarh.

On 1 July, when Linlithgow cabled the result of this conversation to Amery, he proposed that if the Cabinet approved the
concessions that he had foreshadowed, as well as the enlargement of his executive, he would see Maulana A. K. Azad (now
Congress president), Jinnah, and representatives of the princes,
Untouchables, and the Hindu Mahasabha to ascertain whether
they would join the government. Given a favourable response,
the declaration of intent and invitation to co-operate in the war
effort should be issued. Linlithgow had now faced squarely the
alternatives of either attempting a generous accommodation with
Congress, which, if it failed, would at least win over public
opinion, or standing fast without Indian support in the face of
public opinion. Just as in autumn 1939 he had first rejected,
then accepted, the idea of adding non-official Indians to his
Council, so now in summer 1940 he was prepared to concede
what he had resisted for seven months. Amery expressed to
Zetland his delight that Linlithgow had now 'come round very
markedly to our point of view'.[1]

Amery knew that he would have no easy task convincing
Churchill's War Cabinet of the need for a new declaration of
intent. He was proposing no less than full and immediate post-
war dominionhood, provided Indians could agree upon a constitution. He redrafted the offer that Linlithgow had put to

[1] Letter, 1 July 1940, Z.C.

Gandhi, giving more prominence to this point and somewhat
less to the obligations to be included in an Instrument of Agreement or Treaty. In his Cabinet memorandum he stressed that
while Britain had previously promised dominionhood, 'so long
as we indicate neither date nor method, we remain open to the
charge that we are insincere and are merely playing for time,
and until we do so our exhortations to Indians to agree amongst
themselves meet with no response and only add to the suspicion
that we are deliberately procrastinating'.[1] As he impressed upon
Churchill, it was a great advance to promise acceptance of
Dominion status on the basis of whatever agreement Indians
might reach on a constitutional settlement, instead of saying:
'If you agree we may some day do something about it.'[2]

Amery counted on the support of Halifax and the two Labour
members of the War Cabinet (Attlee and Greenwood) but anticipated difficulty with Churchill and Simon. He asked Attlee to
sound out Simon. Attlee had been a member of Simon's Indian
Statutory Commission. He was to write of him: 'He had
immense learning and a brilliant intellect, but a most irresolute
character. He was at his best when a decision had not to be
made.'[3] The judgement is supported by Simon's behaviour on
this occasion. He wrote to Amery that though he had never
ceased to regret the Irwin–Labour Dominion status declaration
of 1929, he would 'be willing enough to get the whole-hearted
support of India for the war now by any reassurance of what we
really mean to do, or to help India to do, when victory is won'.[4]
Amery took this as an intimation of support. But when the
Cabinet met on 12 July Simon left him 'in the lurch', having
by then decided that the problem of the princes must be solved
before a dominion could emerge. Churchill opposed any new
declaration of intent, and his diehard Colonial Secretary, Lord
Lloyd, abhorred any move that might unite Hindu and Muslim
against Britain. With Halifax absent, only Attlee supported
Amery, though Chamberlain intervened to enable him to withdraw his draft declaration for resubmission in a form that
restored Linlithgow's emphasis upon Britain's obligations.

[1] Cabinet memo., 6 July 1940, L/PO/6/105d.
[2] Amery to Churchill, 14 July 1940, ibid.
[3] 'As It Happened', loc. cit.
[4] Letter, 6 July 1940, L/PO/6/105d.

Churchill now took matters into his own hands. He cabled direct to Linlithgow to question the wisdom of any declaration when the invasion of Britain seemed imminent and a parliamentary discussion of 'the issues involved in such a far reaching departure was impossible'.[1]

Linlithgow's position underwent yet another reversal. He replied to Churchill that he had been led so far by Amery's entreaties, which suggested Cabinet support for a declaration that went beyond past statements. Now that he knew of the Cabinet's reservations he would send home a fresh draft. It would still concede that Britain's object was Dominion status within a year of the end of the war and that Indians should frame their own constitution. But it would play down the change of approach, emphasize Britain's obligations, and omit the reference to a treaty. The last point was the most serious loss, for it implied equality of status between Britain and an Indian Dominion.

On 25 July, when Linlithgow's revise came before the Cabinet, Churchill rebuked Amery for going behind his colleagues' backs and misleading them into the belief that the initiative had come from the Viceroy. He had called for all of Amery's correspondence with Linlithgow to be made available to ministers. Amery felt aggrieved, with some justice. Certainly he had expressed his views vigorously to Linlithgow without discussing them in Cabinet, but this was common practice in the 'private' correspondence between Viceroy and Secretary of State. Furthermore, he had not claimed Cabinet backing. Linlithgow must surely have realized that Churchill and Simon would have reservations about his proposed concessions. Indeed, he had explicitly foreshadowed the possibility of Cabinet opposition. He had also related his move to the fall of France and its effect in creating a favourable climate of opinion in India. However, more important than this dispute was the Cabinet's decision at the 25 July meeting to invite Churchill to remodel Linlithgow's draft.

Five days later the Cabinet considered Churchill's 'suggested remodelling': 'Cabinet would not be able to promise in advance "to accept as a body to frame, on the conclusion of the war, the main structure of the Constitution, any body on which the

[1] Cable, 16 July 1940, ibid.

representatives of the principal elements in India's national
life can meantime themselves agree".'[1] Britain must know
beforehand what the body was to be. Further: 'It would be
quite impossible to pledge in advance the attitude of a future
Parliament called into being in the unforeseeable conditions
which will follow the war. Parliament must remain free to use
its judgement and authority on the problems of that future day
in the light of the then existing circumstances.' So much for
India's right to frame its own constitution. Churchill also
expunged the reference to the year's time limit for Dominion
status. He merely provided for Britain to assist the creation,
with the least possible delay after the war, of a body to devise a
constitution, which should be primarily the responsibility of
Indians themselves. The right of India to frame its constitution,
the time limit for Dominion status, and the symbol of India's
equality, the treaty, all were lost now. So was Amery's explic-
ation of a Dominion as a partner-member of the Commonwealth.

As promulgated on 8 August, the Viceroy's offer emphasized
continuity with past policy, as expressed in October 1939, that
the future object was Dominion status, and that the present offer
was the enlargement of the Viceroy's council to include party
representatives and the establishment of a war Consultative
Committee. Britain's obligations to the minorities were spelled
out in a passage that the Muslims were to cling to as a pledge:
'It goes without saying that [His Majesty's Government]
could not contemplate the transfer of their present responsibilities for the peace and welfare of India to any system of
government whose authority is directly denied by large and
powerful elements in India's national life.'[2]

Though Amery tried to make the best of it[3] the offer was not
surprisingly rejected by all parties. The All-India Congress
Committee concluded that Britain had 'no intention to recognise India's independence, and would, if they could, continue to
hold this country indefinitely in bondage for British exploit-

[1] War Cabinet, 30 July 1940, W.P. (40) 295, including Churchill to Linlithgow,
28 July 1940 (cable), ibid.
[2] The British government's offer of 8 Aug. 1940, Gwyer and Appadorai,
Documents, ii. 504–5.
[3] Amery to Zetland, 3 Aug. 1940, Z.C.

ation'.[1] The Viceroy advised, and the Cabinet agreed, that in
the circumstances he should not proceed to enlarge his council
or set up the Consultative Committee.

After a year of war the Viceroy now decided to rely upon
bureaucratic government. On 8 August he wrote to the provincial Governors that with regard to the Revolutionary Movements Ordinance, on whose operation they had been briefed a
few days earlier, 'the situation primarily envisaged is still a clash
with Congress'.[2] In April the Home Department of the Government of India had proposed 'not merely to reduce the Congress
to a condition in which they will be prepared to make terms
but to crush the Congress finally as a political organization'.[3]
Now the Viceroy wrote: 'I feel very strongly that the only
possible answer to a "declaration of war" by any section of
Congress in present circumstances must be a declared determination to crush the organization as a whole.'

Early in September, when Congress authorized Gandhi to
inaugurate a civil disobedience campaign, Linlithgow cabled
home for permission to enact the Revolutionary Movements
Ordinance. In accordance with Amery's recommendation the
Cabinet decided that 'if comprehensive action against Congress
should become inevitable it would be desirable if possible for
public confidence both here and abroad to represent reason for
our action against Congress movement as their programme of
obstruction of war effort and not their political aspirations'.
The Ordinance was 'primarily directed against movement . . .
ostensibly political in character' and the Cabinet was concerned that 'if conflict with Congress should arise, it should
appear as an outcome of war necessity rather than as a political
quarrel unrelated to the war'.[4] In the event Gandhi declined to
court the destruction of his movement by commencing mass
civil disobedience. Instead he launched individual satyagraha
on the issue of freedom to speak against the war, which could

[1] A.I.C.C. Resolution, 15–16 Sept. 1940, Gwyer and Appadorai, *Documents*, ii.
505–6.
[2] Home Pol. (I), 6/13/40, Indian National Archives, quoted in F. Hutchins,
Spontaneous Revolution: The Quit India Movement (Delhi, 1971), 190–1.
[3] Maxwell to P.S.V., 25 Apr. 1940, Home Pol. (I), 3/13/40, in Hutchins, ibid.
190.
[4] War Cabinet, 14 Sept. 1940, W.P. (G) (40) 237, L/PO/6/105d; Amery's
cables of 13, 17, 18 Sept., cited in Hutchins, *Spontaneous Revolution*, 201. See also
D. A. Low, *Lion Rampant* (1973), 163–72.

not be construed as a revolution to obstruct the war effort. The Ordinance was shelved.

Gandhi's relative forbearance and the home government's unwillingness to sanction a campaign to crush Congress as a political organization made possible the reopening of the constitutional issue at a later stage during the war.

(iii) Congress and Co-operation

The recourse of Congress to the futile gesture of individual satyagraha for free speech is a measure of the failures of both the Congress leaders and the British policy-makers during the first year of war. The resignation of provincial office was an impulsive expression of contempt for a Viceroy and a Cabinet that withheld due recognition of the importance of Congress in India's national life. In the past it might have been followed by a heroic mass civil disobedience movement for freedom. But in the context of 1939–40 such a course was impracticable. In the first place, prominent Congressmen wished not to impede Britain in an anti-Fascist war. In the second place, the strength of communal feeling meant that any satyagraha was in danger of being shown up as a Hindu, rather than a national, campaign. A Viceroy and a Cabinet less preoccupied with the purely imperial aspect of the Indian problem would have better appreciated the Congress dilemma and realized that among the party leaders were many who sincerely wanted to cooperate.

The agonizing paralysis of the Congress Working Committee is eloquently revealed in the proceedings of its meeting at Wardha from 15 to 19 April, some three weeks after the Ramgarh and Lahore resolutions:

Gandhiji said that the letters he was receiving from all over the country indicated that there was no atmosphere for the starting of the struggle. In Bengal and Punjab, the struggle will not be against the British but against the respective ministries. . . .

Shri Jawaharlal [Nehru said] Government wants to see how far it can go without exciting us to action. . . . He asked Gandhiji what he would do if he got 50,000 satyagrahis

Gandhiji's reply was that even then communal and other difficulties may make action difficult. He wanted the members to consider the question of the struggle in connection with the attitude of the Muslim League. . . .

Rajendra Babu [said] . . . the recent resolution of the League meant civil war. . . . Any conflict with the British Government would . . . indirectly be a quarrel with the Muslim League. . . . Under such circumstances any mass C.D. would mean civil war. . . .

Profulla Babu was of the opinion that there was no atmosphere for C.D. in the country. In Bengal specially C.D. would mean riot and bloodshed. . . .

Shri Shankarrao Deo's opinion was that though the general atmosphere in the country was not favourable to the starting of C.D. yet no action at this stage would mean demoralization of the rank and file of Congressmen. Something therefore must be done. . . .

Shri Vallabhbhai Patel was of the opinion that unless some sort of action was taken there was bound to be demoralization. . . .

Shri Rajagopalachari was definitely of the view that there was no atmosphere for a fight. The Congress must not be obsessed with the idea of prestige in deciding the issue. If it had gone too fast, it must retrace its steps. Its demands must be modulated. . . .

Mr. Asaf Ali thought that . . . the majority of the Muslims were with the League. . . .

Shri Patwardhan thought that if the fight did not begin the Congress would lose its hold even on the Hindus. . . .

Shri Kripalani said . . . that there was little chance of our getting at the goal by the struggle. It would be undertaken to keep up the morale. . . .

Gandhiji . . . thought there could be no mass C.D. . . . It was possible that Congress may succeed if it started the movement, that is the Government may accede to Congress demands. But that today will only mean that the Muslims are ignored. He did not want such a settlement or such a Swaraj. . . . He was not prepared to say that the League did not represent the Muslim mind. If Muslims want separatism, he will not oppose.[1]

None of the Working Committee saw civil disobedience as a constructive policy. At best it might lift morale, but it would exacerbate communal feeling. In the event the Committee was soon to agree with Rajaji: the way forward was to 'retrace our steps'—British statemanship permitting!

In mid-June, when it met at Wardha, the Committee rejected Gandhi's proposal to extend the creed of non-violence to

---

[1] Proceedings of C.W.C., Wardha, 16–19 Apr. 1940, A.I.C.C. G. 32/1940. I am indebted to Dr. B. R. Tomlinson for this reference. The extracts quoted above are a severely truncated version of this vital document.

national defence. On 21 June it accepted Rajaji's view that, with the fall of France, 'The problem of the achievement of the national freedom has now to be considered along with the one of its maintenance and the defence of the country against the possible external and internal disorder.'[1] On 7 July the Committee accompanied its demand for independence with a new proposal: '. . . as an immediate step in giving effect to it, a provisional National Government should be constituted at the Centre, which, though formed as a transitory measure, should be such as to command the confidence of all the elected elements in the Central Legislature, and secure the closest co-operation of the responsible Governments in the Provinces.'[2] The resolution was confirmed by the All-India Congress Committee. Here was another opportunity of the kind that Nehru believed to exist in August–September 1939, and which he again supported, for Britain and Congress to find agreement within the wider framework of the international situation. Certainly, opinion in the Congress was volatile and Gandhi, apparently set aside for a moment, was soon able to swing a majority of the Working Committee against a policy of co-operating with the war effort. But British policy scarcely gave them a practicable alternative.

(iv) Churchillism

During the year following the failure of the August offer there were some 23,000 convictions under the Defence of India Act. However, the policy of unrelieved repression could not stand alone for long. In March 1941 Sir T. B. Sapru, at a gathering of moderates at Bombay, called for the reconstruction of the Viceroy's executive as an Indianized provisional national government. In the House of Commons official policy was criticized, while opinion was stirring in America. On 22 May, in order to rally moderate support, Linlithgow proposed to set up the long-promised advisory National Defence Council and to increase the Indian membership of his Council. Churchill's immediate response was adverse. The concession

---

[1] Quoted in D. G. Tendulkar, *Mahatma*, V. 286.
[2] Gwyer and Appadorai, *Documents*, ii. 500–1.

of portfolios to Indians would neither advance the war effort nor buy off opposition, but it might engender fresh controversy. Under pressure from Amery, he agreed to rephrase a negative reply in interrogatory form, but wrote to Amery:

In your letter to me of 30 May . . . you say 'Linlithgow's proposals are the least with which I can continue to hold the House of Commons'. This ought not to be the criterion for governing India. I may add that I should find no difficulty in riddling these proposals in Debate to the satisfaction of the overwhelming majority of Members, whether of the Right or the Left.[1]

This time Linlithgow stuck to his guns and Amery, after working behind the scenes for the support of Attlee, Anderson, and Simon, secured the approval of the Cabinet in June. The importance attached to American opinion was indicated by a proposal of Ernest Bevin's to add an Indian Labour Member to the executive. The move would be popular in America, and 'you are concerned about the effect on the United States of this step'.[2]

As reconstructed in summer 1941 the Viceroy's executive included the Commander-in-Chief, the three official British members—for Home, Finance, and Communications—and eight Indians. For the first time Indians formed the majority of the Council. However, the constitution of the Government of India remained unchanged. No portfolio was actually transferred to Indians. The Viceroy retained his special responsibilities for peace and tranquillity, financial stability, the minorities, etc. in respect of which he was required to act in accordance with his individual judgement. The National Defence Council was set up on an advisory basis 'to bring the war effort in the Provinces and the States as well as in the ranks of commerce, industry and labour into more direct and effective touch with the Central Government'.[3] It contained twenty-two British Indians, mostly drawn from the provincial legislatures, and nine states' members.

The reformed executive's first action was to propose the release of those who had been imprisoned for their part in

[1] Letter, 31 May 1941, L/PO/6/105d.
[2] E. Bevin to Amery, 11 June 1941, Bevin Collection 3/1, Churchill College, Cambridge.
[3] Amery's speech in House of Commons, 1 Aug. 1941.

Gandhi's individual satyagraha. All of the Indian and two of
the European members supported the step. Linlithgow did
not expect it to effect a change of heart in Congress, but he
thought the release innocuous and he was reluctant to risk
resignations from his reformed council by exercising his power
to override the opinion of the majority. Churchill disliked this
apparent surrender to Congress. However, the Cabinet favoured
the release, which took place in December.

Though Churchill conceded both the reconstruction of the
executive and the release of the satyagrahis, he was utterly
immovable when the question of Britain's aims in relation to
India re-emerged. The occasion was his parliamentary speech
on the Roosevelt–Churchill Atlantic Charter, signed at sea in
August 1941. Article 3 expressed 'the right of all peoples to
choose the form of government under which they will live'. It
was significant that not even the advice of the U.S. ambassador,
Guy Winant, to whom he sent a copy of his proposed speech,
could influence him. Winant believed that the passage denying
the application of the article to India 'would simply intensify
charges of Imperialism and leave Great Britain in the position
of "a do-nothing policy" '.[1] Churchill refused to modify the
passage. On 9 September he told the House of Commons that
the article applied only to European nations under Nazi rule.
It did not relate to 'the development of constitutional government in India, Burma or other parts of the Empire'. The 'progressive evolution of self-governing institutions in the regions
and peoples who owe allegiance to the British Crown' was to be
distinguished from the emancipation of Europe from Nazism.

Churchill cited the August 1940 offer as the definitive statement of British aims in India. He was, in effect, reaffirming his
cabled advice to Linlithgow after the failure of the offer:
'Declaration represented the farthest Cabinet was prepared to
go.'[2] One so moderate as Sapru said of that declaration:

[It] has given rise to grave misgivings and has caused a great deal of
resentment. . . . Hedged in by so many conditions [it] is so incom-
plete in the enunciation of the aim [of British rule] and so non-com-

---

[1] Winant to Secretary of State (Cordell Hull), 4 Nov. 1941, *Foreign Relations of
the United States: Diplomatic Papers*, 1941, iii. 181–2.
[2] Cable, 14 Aug. 1940, L/PO/6/105d.

mittal in regard to its being implemented within any reasonable distance of time that it can afford no satisfaction whatever to the people of this country.[1]

In the wake of Churchill's Atlantic Charter speech resentment was turning to bitterness. Moderates with long memories could not recall a wider gulf between Britain and India than that which emerged after two years of war.

In mid-November 1939 Cripps had written to Nehru of a 'quite remarkable change of opinion [on India], even amongst Conservatives, which is most remarkable'.[2] He thought the Churchill view 'definitely in a very small minority now', and apart from Churchill's influence in Cabinet 'not influential otherwise'. The fact was that with the collapse of the paper federation the distinction between Churchill's views and Cabinet policy became elusive. The failure of the federation proposal enhanced Churchill's supremacy, while some of the odium of the policy of appeasing Hitler attached to the conciliatoriness of Halifax and Hoare in relation to India. There was, in effect, no official constitutional policy to deal with the problem of India's unity and freedom.

The Viceroy failed to give the Cabinet a firm lead and made himself an easy target by his vacillation: by immediately suspending and then reviving the federation idea; by first denying and later admitting the desirability of enlarging the Indian element in his executive; by initially opposing and finally espousing the scheme for a constituent assembly and a treaty; and by wavering over the advantage of calling a small conference of Indians together. Like the non-Labour ministers in Cabinet his primary concern was for Britain's imperial interests; like them, too, he succumbed to the superior force of Churchill, who never doubted that the imperial interest would be best served by yielding nothing at all.

The only substantial alternative to a do-nothing policy was a fresh initiative for Indian freedom and unity, based upon negotiations with the Indian parties. Such an alternative came from Cripps alone, and his ideas lay behind the only constructive approaches that were made during the first two years of

[1] Sapru's statement, 1–2 Nov. 1941, Gwyer and Appadorai, *Documents*, ii. 518.
[2] Letter, 16 Nov. 1939, J.N. Coll.

war: the Zetland proposals of December 1939–March 1940, and the suggestions of Amery's that gave rise to the adulterated offer of August 1940.

Broadly speaking, the contrasting influences on policy were Churchillian negativism and Crippsian constructiveness. With Cripps a minor political figure, absent from London for almost the whole of the early war years, and with India of relatively little significance for the war, Churchill tamed his adversaries with relative ease. By September 1941 the horizons of British policy did not extend beyond 'Churchillism'.

3

THE SECOND OFFER
(October 1941–March 1942)

(i) Towards a Labour Initiative

IN OCTOBER 1941 Sir George Schuster represented to Amery the views of an all-party group of parliamentarians who were impatient with the 'purely negative policy'.[1] The group included Sir Edward Cadogan, Lord Pethick-Lawrence, Sir John Wardlaw Milne, and Mr. Graham White. Their suggested line of action resembled that of Cripps in May 1940: send out a parliamentary mission 'to get the Indian Party leaders down to the hard brain work of discussing the details of a new constitution'.[2] Linlithgow rebuffed the idea.

After the Japanese attack on Pearl Harbour on 7 December pressures were exerted from several directions for a new initiative. India was now a vital base for operations in the Pacific and South-east Asia. Within a month Churchill had received approaches from three main quarters: the Labour members of his Cabinet; the President of the United States; and Sapru and the moderates.

The influence behind the first Labour initiative was the India Conciliation Group. The Group had kept in touch with Cripps until his departure for Russia. Agatha Harrison remained in communication with Lady Cripps, and when they met early in December 1941 for a long talk Miss Harrison 'said how much [she] hoped that Sir Stafford could go to India'.[3] On 15 December she sent Lady Cripps a letter on the situation, proposing the formation of a national government, which she

[1] Letter, 6 Nov. 1941, L/PO/77.
[2] Schuster to Amery, 25 Nov. 1941, ibid.
[3] Confidential note by A. Harrison, 27 Jan. 1942, I.C.G., Cripps file.

thought Cripps might be able to bring about. Copies were dispatched to Cripps himself and to *The Times*, which reported a (groundless) rumour that he would visit India *en route* home from Russia. The letter regretted the lack of personal contact between Britain and India during the war, except for Cripps's visit in 1939, and was critical of Linlithgow's isolation from Congress. He had never met Azad (the president), had met Nehru for the first time in 1938 in London through the mediation of the Conciliation Group, and only once subsequently (in October 1939). He had not seen Gandhi for over a year.

In a letter of 18 December to I.C.G. colleagues Miss Harrison remarked that she was testing out on a few people the idea of a Cripps visit to India:

Sir Stafford is a man of integrity—understands Nehru—can move easily between all. No hesitation interferes when military commanders can not achieve results—why cannot this method apply to India. The prestige of the Viceroy may be a factor in all this; yet Younghusband said Amery felt someone was needed to bring the parties together. He thought of Wedgwood Benn—Sir Stafford would be infinitely better. It is rumoured he may come back. Then let him pick up the threads here—and go immediately to India for a few weeks.[1]

One of Miss Harrison's contacts was Arthur Creech-Jones, parliamentary secretary to Ernest Bevin, Minister for Labour and National Service: 'Creech-Jones asked me to brief him for his Minister. Happily I had an editorial that mentioned Bevin —saying that he was the only man who could stand up to Churchill—but that he Bevin—was giving no thought to India.'[2] This was not quite true. In September Bevin had raised the Indian question with Amery and followed up with a letter:

I must confess that leaving the settlement of the Indian problem until after the war fills me with alarm. . . . We made certain definite promises in the last war and practically a quarter of a century has gone, and, though there has been an extension of self-government, we have not, in my view, 'delivered the goods' in a broad and

[1] Letter to C. Heath, A. Wilson, H. Alexander, I.C.G., Cripps file. Sir Francis Younghusband, formerly of the Indian Political Service, was a sometime member of the I.C.G.
[2] Ibid.

generous way. It is quite understandable that neither Muslim nor Hindu places much confidence in our 'after war promises'. It seems to me that the time to take action to establish Dominion Status is now—to develop or improvise the form of Government to carry us through the war but to remove from all doubt the question of Indian freedom at the end of the war. I firmly believe that a bold step now would rally Indian opinion behind us.[1]

With Churchill absent on a visit to Washington, Attlee presided over a War Cabinet meeting on 19 December at which Bevin

said that he thought there was some anxiety in this country about the position in India, both from the point of view of defence and of the Constitutional issue. For example, was our policy calculated to get the fullest war effort from India? . . . He thought that the position might give rise to a demand for a discussion in Parliament at short notice, and that it might therefore be desirable that the War Cabinet should have a general discussion on the position at the first convenient opportunity.[2]

The Cabinet conclusions were sent on to Churchill.

While Churchill was in Washington (22 December 1941–14 January 1942) Roosevelt raised the question of Indian reform with him. Churchill recorded that he 'reacted so strongly and at such length that [Roosevelt] never raised it verbally again'.[3] If Churchill's usage of 'verbally' was correct then his remark is misleading. Roosevelt's intervention did not stop there.

American interest in the Indian problem had been growing. In April 1941 Halifax, now ambassador to the U.S.A., proposed to the State Department the attachment of an Indian to the British Embassy, with the title 'Agent-General for India in the United States'.[4] The U.S. Secretary of State saw no objection to the appointment but used the opportunity to emphasize 'the present inadequacy of American representation in India occasioned by the unwillingness of the Government of India to permit representatives of the Government of the United States to reside or to maintain offices in the capital city of

[1] Bevin to Amery, 24 Sept. 1941, Bevin Coll. 3/1.
[2] War Cabinet, 19 Dec. 1941, W.M. 131 (41) 4, N. Mansergh and E. W. R. Lumby (eds.), *The Transfer of Power, 1942–7, Vol. I, The Cripps Mission* (1970), 6 n. Hereafter referred to as C.M. References are to document numbers.
[3] W. S. Churchill, *Hinge of Fate* (1951), 209.
[4] British Embassy to Department of State, 17 Apr. 1941, FRUS, 1941, iii, 170.

Delhi', which was a thousand miles from the principal American Consular Office in Calcutta.[1] He proposed that an American Foreign Service Officer of minister rank should be permitted to reside in Delhi. In July the exchange of representatives was announced. Sir G. S. Bajpai took up office in Washington and Mr. T. M. Wilson, the Commissioner designate, presented his letters of credence to the Viceroy before the motion-picture cameras in the great Durbar Hall in New Delhi.

In May 1941 A. A. Berle, the Assistant Secretary of State, took the first step towards American interference with British constitutional policy in India. He wrote an *aide-mémoire*, which he agreed might seem 'sensational', suggesting that the importance of India as a source of manpower and materials for the war in the Middle East was such that an effort should be made to convert her into an active rather than a passive ally: 'To that end the Government of the United States hopes that His Majesty's Government will promptly explore the possibility of bringing India into the partnership of nations on terms equal to the other members of the British Common-wealth.'[2] On 7 May the Secretary of State, Cordell Hull, inquired orally of Halifax whether, in view of its problems in Iraq and Iran, Britain 'found it feasible to consider further acts of liberalizing the relations of the United Kingdom to India'.[3] Halifax replied that Indian sentiment towards Britain was very good, that the Hindus and the Muslims were at odds with each other, and that further liberalizing concessions were neither feasible nor necessary.

On 1 August Guy Winant advised Hull of a matter that would soon come up for discussion: Australia and New Zealand were disturbed by Japanese encroachments and wanted the U.S.A. and Britain to recognize their situation and further their security. Winant reflected:

It occurred to me that when this matter was called to your attention it might permit a reference to India. I have thought for some time that the charge of imperialism against England in the United States largely focused on the Indian situation. This sentiment hinders support to Britain. . . . It might be possible at least to get agreement

[1] Secretary of State to British Ambassador, 28 May 1941, ibid. 170–1.
[2] Draft *aide-mémoire* enclosed with Berle's memo., 5 May 1941, ibid. 176–7.
[3] Ibid. 178.

on the right of Dominion status for India so as to eliminate that
major issue now, while at the same time giving a further pledge to
implement this status within a stated period following the cessation
of hostilities. Among other considerations I believe this action would
have a sobering effect upon the Japanese.[1]

Berle drafted a cable to Winant giving presidential approval
for him to raise the question with Churchill and the Foreign
Office. However, on 6 August the Under-Secretary of State,
Mr. Sumner Welles, who had advised in May against doing
'anything which might upset the Indian apple cart',[2] counselled
Hull that the United States was 'not warranted in suggesting
officially to the British Government what the status of India
should be'.[3] If the President were disposed to raise the matter
he would surely 'wish to discuss it in a very personal and
confidential way directly with Mr. Churchill'. According to
Elliott Roosevelt, his father raised the question of India's
economic development with Churchill on board the *Augusta* a
few days later, when the Atlantic Charter was in preparation.
He described Churchill as expostulating to the point of explo-
sion: 'I thought for a minute he was going to bust, Pop.'[4]

In November, following a protest from the Premier of Burma
against the offensive passage in Churchill's reference to article 3
of the Charter, the Chief of the North East Division of the
State Department anticipated 'repercussions in India which
may serve to impede further India's contribution to the war'.[5]
He suggested to Berle and Welles that the President might
now consider recommending to Churchill that Britain grant
Dominion status to India. Welles advised Hull that it was
Halifax's view that an immediate change in India's status
would create internal dissension and thereby impede rather
than advance the war effort. He felt, too, that in view of
Churchill's well-known and frequently published attitude
concerning the status of India such an approach was sure to
be resented.[6] He opposed U.S. intervention 'unless we are

---

[1] Ibid. 178–9.
[2] Ibid. 176 n. 6.
[3] Ibid. 181.
[4] E. Roosevelt, *As He Saw It* (New York, 1946), 35–8.
[5] Memo., 7 Nov. 1941, FRUS, 1941, iii. 184–6.
[6] Welles to Hull, 15 Nov. 1941, ibid. 186–7.

convinced that some step of this character is imperatively required from the standpoint of our own national policy, and of our national defense'. With the attack on Pearl Harbour this condition was fulfilled, but when Roosevelt's personal overture to Churchill in Washington was rebuffed the matter lapsed until after the fall of Singapore (15 February). At the same time, the preparation of the Lend–Lease Agreement early in 1942 gave America a powerful lever in imperial policy, and in January Amery knew that Hull was prepared to use it in relation to imperial tariff preferences.

On 2 January the third main source of pressure on Churchill appeared. Sir T. B. Sapru and twelve other moderates felt compelled, in view of the grave international situation, to appeal to Churchill for 'a bold stroke [of] far-sighted statesmanship'.[1] Their demand was similar to that of the Non-Party leaders in March 1941: the elevation of India to Dominion status at once; the expansion of the central executive into an all-Indian national government responsible directly to the Crown; the restoration of popular government in the provinces; the recognition of India's right of representation in the Imperial War Cabinet (if one were established), in allied war councils, and at the peace conference. The signatories were elder statesmen of distinction, including Lord Sinha, Srinivasa Sastri, M. R. Jayakar, Jagdish Prasad, and Sivaswami Aiyar. They did not include any Congress or League leaders. However, there was evidence of Congress interest in securing access to government.

During the last week of 1941 the Congress Working Committee met for the first time in fourteen months. As in July 1940 it rejected the extension of Gandhi's creed of non-violence to the sphere of national defence. Gandhi now resigned the leadership that had been thrust upon him in September 1940. Though there had been no change of British policy the C.W.C. resolved that it 'must nevertheless take into full consideration the new world situation that has arisen by the development of the war into a world conflict and its approach to India'.[2] Independence and a constituent assembly remained the Congress policy, but the way was open for the party to associate

[1] Cable, C.M., 2.
[2] C.W.C. Resolution, 30 Dec. 1941, C.M., Appx. III.

with the government in the defence of India if suitable opportunity arose.

Churchill's response to these various overtures and reorientations was implacable. In effect, his cable to Attlee from Washington on 7 January acknowledged but rebuffed them:

I hope my colleagues will realize the danger of raising constitutional issue, still more of making constitutional changes, in India at a moment when enemy is upon the frontier. The idea that we should 'get more out of India' by putting the Congress in charge at this juncture seems ill-founded. . . . Bringing hostile political element into the defence machine will paralyse action. Merely picking and choosing friendly Indians will . . . not in any way meet political demands. . . . The Indian troops are fighting splendidly, but it must be remembered that their allegiance is to the King Emperor, and that the rule of the Congress and Hindoo Priesthood machine would never be tolerated by a fighting race. I do not think you will have any trouble with American opinion. . . . Pray communicate these views to the Cabinet. I trust we shall not depart from the position we have deliberately taken up.[1]

Attlee replied that the constitutional issue was sure to be raised in Parliament soon and that if Sapru's appeal were rebuffed his Labour colleagues would find themselves in great difficulty.

On 13 January Amery asked Linlithgow for his views upon a suitable reply to Sapru. He himself favoured Churchill reiterating the August offer. He would also be prepared to 'go a long way in improving the inter-Imperial and international status of India'.[2] But he could not imagine the Indian parties agreeing upon the reallocation of seats in the central government and he was hesitant about reconstructing the body again so soon. He viewed the new quasi-co-operative stance of Congress as an attempt to shift Britain from the determination expressed in the August offer not to advance without agreement among the Indian parties. Yet he was uneasy at Britain's omission to take any initiative to bring the parties together to discuss 'the constitutional future or . . . the more immediate present'. On 16 January he drafted a reply to Sapru's appeal. It reaffirmed the August offer, argued the

---

[1] C.M., 6.   [2] C.M., 11.

past failure of Congress and the League to agree on terms for entering the central executive, and opposed the idea of the executive being converted into a dictatorship of the Viceroy, or a majority of his executive, nominally responsible directly to the Crown.

Linlithgow agreed broadly with Amery. Sapru's proposals were 'a leap in the dark from the solid platform of the Act of 1935',[1] with no guarantee of reward. He denied 'that any entirely non-official Council that I could put together unless it had the full support of the majority parties (who have refrained from supporting Sapru) would be better than I have got at the moment'. As for going further, accepting the demand for full independence and giving present proof of so doing, that was out of the question.

On that assumption we may take it that there is no possibility of giving satisfaction to Congress or securing their real and whole-hearted support. In my experience they are entirely ruthless politicians; will take all they can get; will do their utmost to manœuvre us into a position in which we make sacrifices that are substantial and that will increase the prestige and the power of the Congress in this country. But short of acceptance of their full demand no sacrifices however great can be relied on to keep them quiet.

His general conclusion was that 'we should stand firm and make no further move'. If Indians were given any more power Britain could not rely upon a 'united India . . . solid behind us in fighting the war. India is hopelessly, and I suspect irremediably, split by racial and religious divisions which we cannot bridge, and which become more acute as any real transfer of power by us draws nearer.'

Linlithgow's long dispatch embellished his appreciation with an excursus into imperialist philosophy:

I know that we are frequently urged to do something to 'touch the heart' of India and our sympathies naturally lean in that direction. But Cabinet will I think agree with me that India and Burma have no natural association with the Empire, from which they are alien by race, history and religion, and for which as such neither of them have any natural affection, and both are in the Empire because they are conquered countries which had been brought there by force

[1] Linlithgow to Amery, 21 Jan. 1942, C.M., 23.

[and] kept there by our controls. . . . I suspect that the moment they think that we may lose the war or take a bad knock, their leaders would be much more concerned to make terms with the victor at our expense than to fight for the ideals to which so much lip-service is given. . . . What we have to decide . . . is whether in such circumstances, whatever the feeling of India, we intend to stay in this country for our own reasons. . . . If we accept that India is too important at this stage for us to take any chances, then I would rather face such trouble as we may have to face here as a result of making no concessions now in the political field than make concessions.

Linlithgow appealed direct to Churchill for support on a policy of 'standing firm and facing the music'.[1] Amery supported his judgement. There was 'nothing to be done at this moment'.[2] He sent copies of Linlithgow's appreciation to Churchill, Attlee, Simon, and Anderson.

Attlee found the dispatch distinctly disturbing.[3] It assumed Congress 'solidarity in intransigence', whereas he 'had the impression that a good many of them were looking for a way out of the impasse of their own creation'. He thought Linlithgow sounded defeatist and he questioned his judgement, suggesting that other opinions be sought, for example that of the Chief Justice, Sir Maurice Gwyer. Recently Attlee had proposed seconding Gwyer to inquire into the constitutional problem. He insisted that some action was necessary:

It is worth considering [he wrote to Amery] whether someone should not be charged with a mission to try to bring the political leaders together. There is a lot of opinion here which we cannot ignore which is not satisfied that there is nothing to be done, but to sit tight on the declaration of August 1940. This opinion exists in your Party as well as mine.

Amery replied that Congress was solidly intransigent in its opposition to the August offer's requirement that the future constitution must be settled by agreement between the parties. It was hopelessly negative.[4] He too had found 'one or two things in the tone of Linlithgow's telegram not altogether to

[1] Linlithgow to Churchill, 21 Jan. 1942, C.M., 26.
[2] Amery to Churchill, 22 Jan. 1942, C.M., 27.
[3] Attlee to Amery, 24 Jan. 1942, C.M., 35.
[4] Amery to Attlee, 26 Jan. 1942, C.M., 38.

[his] liking' but he saw no prospect of a constitutional step that would bring the parties together or help the war effort. The only possible emissary was himself. Neither Churchill nor Linlithgow would favour such a course unless emergency defence measures and political mediation made it necessary. Attlee remained unconvinced, noting on 27 January that the position was 'most unsatisfactory and I very much doubt whether it can be held'.[1]

Attlee was reflecting opinion in his party. On 22 January the Labour M.P. and chairman of the India League, R. W. Sorensen, told Agatha Harrison that the Labour Party wanted Cripps, who was to return to London the next day, to go to India with powers to effect a settlement. She noted that it was 'rather fun when he told me as though it was quite a new idea'.[2] Throughout the month she had been concentrating upon the 'send a special envoy scheme'. Her analysis of the recent resolutions of the Indian parties led her to conclude that there was a common denominator on which parties might be brought to agree: 'that of common dissatisfaction with the government at the Centre and wanting this to be truly responsible as an interim measure'.[3] She was encouraged by the Indian Reuter correspondent's opinion that an influential mediator was required. She fed appropriate papers to Geoffrey Wilson and Lady Cripps. On the morning of 26 January Lady Cripps phoned to ask her to send around urgently a copy of Cripps's 1939 scheme.[4] Besides the copy, that day Cripps received a letter from Carl Heath, chairman of the I.C.G., written at Miss Harrison's request.

Heath's letter brought together two facts. First, Indians were

open to the direct, personal as 'equal to equal' relationship, and give thereto a warm response once they feel that freedom and democracy are *meant* by the man who speaks to them for this country. That at present they do *not* believe, either of Amery or Linlithgow. . . . [The Viceroy was] an upright, sincere over cautious slow elder of the Scottish Kirk: but in spite of his sincerity he cannot reach the Indian leaders, for behind his own caution lies the heavy hand of

[1] To Amery, 27 Jan. 1942, C.M., 42.
[2] Harrison to Heath, 23 Jan. 1942, I.C.G., Cripps file.
[3] Harrison to Heath, 4 Jan. 1942, ibid.
[4] I.C.G. Notes, 26 Jan. 1942.

Whitehall, with its constant talk of its 'ultimate goal', and its entire lack of personal and direct touch with, and sympathetic understanding of, Indian leaders and their ardent national desires.

And second, all parties were 'concentrating on the immediate question of a National Government—that is the transfer of real power to the Viceroy's Council so that the Council becomes a genuine Government whose advice the Viceroy will follow'. The two points taken together suggested 'a situation ripe for the new and healing hand. . . . At this moment many believe that _you_ are the man. To pacify and consolidate free India would be an immense and untold service. I beg you to consider it.'[1] At this time Cripps was still only a non-party member of the House of Commons. Nevertheless, he returned from Moscow with immense personal prestige and popularity. He was widely, though falsely, associated with the Russian entry into the war as an ally, and he enjoyed some reflected glory from the Russians' heroic resistance to the German invasion. It seems reasonable to assume that he was in touch with Attlee at the end of January.

On 2 February Attlee set down for the War Cabinet a memorandum on the Indian political situation. It contested the conclusion of Linlithgow and Amery that 'nothing can or should be done at the present time', which resulted from 'a dangerous ignoring of the present situation'.[2] Britain could no longer afford a Eurocentric view of the world. It had been necessary to form a co-operative alliance with China and 'semi-oriental' Russia against an Asiatic nation enjoying success in opposition to Britain and America. The changed relation between Europeans and Asiatics must be reflected in Britain's relations with India, if Britain was not to store up trouble for the future. The formation of a pan-Asiatic bloc of Britain's allies was possible in the post-war world. The Viceroy's reference to India and Burma as an alien and conquered element in the Empire was astonishing, reading like 'an extract from an anti-imperialist propaganda speech'. It was a great achievement of British rule to have planted in India British principles of justice and liberty, the very 'ethical conceptions'

[1] Heath to Cripps, 26 Jan. 1942, I.C.G., Cripps file.
[2] C.M., 60.

upon which India's condemnation of that rule were based. Britain should appeal to the principles of democracy and liberty to rally Indians to the war for a common cause. The Viceroy's crude imperialism was unacceptable. A do-nothing policy might enable Britain to weather the present storm. But 'what of subsequent storms? Such a hand-to-mouth policy is not statesmanship.' Now was 'the time for an act of statesmanship. To mark time is to lose India. A renewed effort must be made to get the leaders of the Indian political parties to unite. It is quite obvious from his telegram that the Viceroy is not the man to do this. Indeed, his telegram goes far to explain his past failures.' The alternatives open were to entrust a person of standing with wide powers to negotiate a settlement in India, or to bring over Indian representatives to discuss a settlement. The first seemed to offer greater flexibility in negotiations. The chosen representative would have 'very wide powers both as to the future and as to the present', though the latter seemed less important than the former:

There is a precedent for such action. Lord Durham saved Canada to the British Empire. We need a man to do in India what Durham did in Canada. . . . A representative with power to negotiate within wide limits should be sent to India now, either as a special envoy or in replacement of the present Viceroy, and . . . a Cabinet Committee should be appointed to draw up terms of reference and powers.

(ii) The Hardliners Give Ground

The battle of policies and philosophies that appeared in the Linlithgow and Attlee analyses of the position was soon joined in the War Cabinet. Both analyses were placed before it on 5 February. Anderson and Amery favoured a do-nothing approach to the constitutional problem while Attlee, and no doubt Bevin, wanted a fresh initiative. Amery reported the proceedings to Linlithgow:

We . . . came on to the proposed reply to Sapru but after starting the discussion of that it was suggested that it could only be dealt with in the light of our decision on the major issue of policy, *i.e.*, whether the Cabinet should do what I recommended, namely, make the most of the authority and *izzat* of your new Executive and of the N[ational] D[efence] C[ouncil] but otherwise stand pat for the time being till we saw a better opportunity for bringing the parties together, or considering Attlee's demand that we should take some definite step now towards breaking the deadlock. After a good deal of ragging of his Labour colleagues, with an occasional eye-wink at me, Winston suddenly propounded [his] great scheme.[1]

Another observer, Sir Alexander Cadogan, noted that after a lively discussion Churchill 'floored everyone by announcing *his* remedy'.[2] His intervention was, for the moment, to take the edge off the Cabinet division and elbow aside the scheme for an emissary.

Churchill's scheme, which Amery was left to draft with the help of Attlee and Anderson, was to expand the Defence Council into an elective body of one hundred, representing the provincial assemblies and the princes, and to extend its functions. Not only would the Council discuss the war effort; after the war it would be the body to frame the new constitution. In the drafting of the scheme, with which Simon (Lord Chancellor but not a War Cabinet member) also assisted, there emerged a clear divergence between Amery and Attlee over the merits of insisting upon the August offer's minorities pledge.

On 11 February Amery cabled to Linlithgow: 'Please take strongest peg you can before continuing.'[3] He went on to say that Churchill proposed to broadcast to India within a few days, appealing for co-operation with his expanded Defence of India Council. Churchill's concern was the product of the deteriorating situation in the East. The Japanese were advancing rapidly in the Pacific and Burma, Singapore was in peril, and it was necessary to placate American and Chinese opinion on India.

Linlithgow was aghast at Churchill going so far without consulting him, and he foreshadowed a 'reasoned criticism' exposing his proposals as 'founded upon a complete failure to comprehend the true nature of our difficulties in India'.[4] The appraisal that he dispatched on 13 February scuttled the scheme: '. . . it precipitates the whole constitutional

---

[1] Amery to Linlithgow, 9 Feb. 1942, C.M., 89.
[2] D. Dilks (ed.), *The Diaries of Alexander Cadogan, 1938–45* (1971), 5 Feb. 1942, 432.
[3] C.M., 101.
[4] Linlithgow to Amery, 12 Feb. 1942, C.M., 103.

controversy, which is so largely communal and on a present view irreconcilable, into the conduct of the war and the day-to-day government of this country'.[1] Neither Congress nor the League would accept the composition of the new body, but if it were set up it would come into conflict with the existing central executive and legislature. The conduct of the war and the framing of a post-war constitution were inappropriate functions for the same body.

Linlithgow destroyed Churchill's plan, but he nevertheless felt aggrieved. The day after Singapore fell he wrote to Amery:

> I am still, for the first time in my life, really cross with you all over this business, and I do again beg of you to see to it that I should be in some measure cushioned by you and your Office from the full impact of these explosions in the Prime Minister's mind. I am carrying here, almost single-handed, an immense responsibility. Indeed, I do not think it is to exaggerate to affirm that the key to success in this war is now very largely in my hands. . . . Let me only tell you that in my careful judgement, the manner in which I have been used over these past ten days is not in tune with the treatment which anyone holding my charge is entitled to expect from His Majesty's Government.[2]

The next day (17 February) Amery asked him for an alternative positive plan which Linlithgow had offered to consider if required. Churchill now sent an interim reply to Sapru, saying that his appeal was still under discussion.

On 19 February Churchill reconstructed the War Cabinet, a step demanded by the British failures in Malaya and Burma. Attlee became Deputy Prime Minister and Secretary of State for Dominion Affairs. Cripps joined the War Cabinet, taking Attlee's former portfolio (Lord Privy Seal), and became Leader of the House of Commons.

The next day Cripps went straight from lunch with Churchill to a meeting with eighteen members of the India Conciliation Group. Horace Alexander was chairman, and Lady Cripps was present. It was 'made abundantly clear that this talk was absolutely private—the fact it had taken place must not be mentioned and no reference to what Sir Stafford said'.[3] Cripps's plan for India was essentially his 1939 scheme (which

---

[1] Linlithgow to Amery, 13 Feb. 1942, C.M., 121.
[2] Linlithgow to Amery, 16 Feb. 1942, C.M., 135.
[3] I.C.G. Notes, 20 Feb. 1942.

he had discussed with the Group in May 1940). In response to his invitation for comment, it was said that while the plan dealt with the long range changes it did not affect the immediate present and the demand for a national government. Cripps felt that 'the body he would like to see set up might do this—as no-one would override the strong views such a body would hold'. However, the executive council would remain. Alexander 'pointed out that any such group would be useless unless the Prime Minister made it clear that the Viceroy would abide by the advice of any newly formed body'. Cripps assured the Group that a real reconstruction of the Viceroy's executive was out of the question.[1] It seems reasonable to assume that he had in mind the introduction of the majority parties' leaders into the executive, which would, however, remain responsible to Parliament in London, with the Viceroy retaining his overriding authority to discharge his special responsibilities.

On 21 February Amery circulated to Churchill, Attlee, Anderson, Simon, and Cripps a copy of an article by Alexander Inglis, *The Times* correspondent in New Delhi. Amery commended it as a very clear statement of the Indian problem: 'how to convince Indians of our sincerity as to the future and how to give them further responsibility at the present time without prejudging the communal issue.'[2] Inglis proposed reconstructing the Viceroy's executive within the existing constitution and retaining the special responsibilities.

Now Amery himself yielded to the pressures to abandon his do-nothing stance and seek a constructive line of advance. His mind was 'crystallizing towards the conclusion' that Britain must be 'more definite both as to time and method' with regard to the future and go substantially further in the present.[3] For the long term Amery favoured a clear statement that within a specific time after the war Britain would endorse a constitution framed by Indians themselves, subject to the negotiation of a treaty. This was to reinstate the initiative of July 1940 that Churchill and Linlithgow had adulterated. But in a vital respect Amery would go much further.

[1] Heath to Harrison, 25 Feb. 1942, I.C.G., Cripps file.
[2] Minute by Amery, 21 Feb. 1942, C.M., 162.
[3] Amery to Linlithgow, 21 Feb. 1942, C.M., 163.

Formerly, Britain had insisted upon the parties' agreement in making a single Dominion constitution, upon, in effect, freedom only with unity. The no-freedom-without-unity policy had been widely condemned as a machiavellian device to justify British rule for the indefinite future. Amery now proposed to silence such criticism by providing that

if there are sufficient Provinces who want to get together and form a Dominion the dissident Provinces should be free to stand out and either come in after a period of option or be set up at the end of it as Dominions of their own. Jinnah could not quarrel with that [for it conceded Pakistan] nor, on the other hand, could Congress feel that it is denied the opportunity of complete independence for that part of India which it controls.

Amery argued that this solution to the problem was consistent with British practice in devolving power upon the white dominions, notably Australia, Canada, and South Africa. It is noteworthy that it was also consistent with Cripps's conclusion in December 1939 that prior to the detailed work of a constituent assembly there must, if the League was to co-operate, be a generally acceptable settlement in outline of the imperial problem.

For the short term, Amery's purely personal preference was to seek a half-way house between an unchanged central executive and Sapru's Indianized national government responsible to the Crown.[1] There were currently two vacancies on the council. A third would be created by sending a representative to the War Cabinet, which had recently been agreed as a concession to national sentiment. A fourth could emerge with the dispatch of an Indian to China as ambassador and a fifth by dropping one of the existing members. In addition, the official Finance Member (J. Raisman) might be transferred to a lesser portfolio, while the Commander-in-Chief might cede defence administration though retaining the defence policy portfolio. Of the six seats thus made available three might be offered to Congress, two to the League, and one to Ambedkar, the Untouchable leader. The Home portfolio would remain with Maxwell, and there would still be three official members.

On 25 February Linlithgow's 'constructive suggestions' arrived. They envisaged no real advance beyond the long-term

[1] Amery to Linlithgow, 22 Feb. 1942, C.M., 165.

policy of the August 1940 offer, though they would 'recognise without delay the *de facto* status of India under a National Government'.[1] Linlithgow would consult Indian political leaders on the reconstruction of his executive. Though he would not promise the elimination of the official members as a prerequisite of a political truce he would discuss that matter 'round the table as a practical problem of administration with such leaders as may emerge as likely to be those from among whom his future colleagues in a National Government will be drawn'. He had in mind the removal of the Home and Finance portfolios from the sphere of political controversy by the appointment of permanent official Advisers reporting direct to himself.[2] He was opposed to the cession of defence administration by the Commander-in-Chief but thought the appointment of an Indian to defence co-ordination might be feasible.

Linlithgow claimed that he had 'gone to utmost limit that my conscience and any Viceroy's capacity to bear the burden will admit'.[3] He was, in effect, contemplating virtually the full Indianization of his executive save for the Commander-in-Chief, though he would reserve Home and Finance to himself. The reformed council would operate within the framework of the existing constitution.

Linlithgow's suggestions were never fully considered. They were overtaken by events. On 26 February a War Cabinet Committee began to consider the form and contents of a new declaration of policy. It was the product of the growing sense of urgency among Churchill's non-Conservative colleagues in the War Cabinet, a renewed appeal from Sapru, and the mounting international pressures of Britain's key allies in the East.

On 21 February, after a fortnight in India during which he met Gandhi and Nehru, the Generalissimo Chiang Kai-shek released from Government House, Calcutta, a message that claimed the sympathy of the vast majority of world opinion for 'India's aspirations for freedom'.[4] It expressed the hope that

[1] Linlithgow to Amery, 25 Feb. 1942, C.M., 183.
[2] Linlithgow to Amery, 26 Feb. 1942, C.M., 184.
[3] Linlithgow to Amery, 25 Feb. 1942, C.M., 183.
[4] Encl. with Linlithgow to Amery, 23 Feb. 1942, C.M., 173.

'our ally Great Britain [would] without waiting for any demands on part of people of India . . . as speedily as possible give
them real political power so that they may be in position
further to develop their spiritual and material strength and
thus realize that their participation in war is . . . turning
point in their struggle for India's freedom'. On the 24th Chiang
sent a cable to his ambassador in London, with a copy to his
Minister for Foreign Affairs in Washington, to say that he had
been 'personally shocked by the Indian military and political
situation':

. . . if the Indian political problem is not immediately and urgently
solved, the danger will be daily increasing. If the British Government should wait until Japanese planes begin to bomb India and
the Indian morale collapses it would already be too late. . . . If the
Japanese should know of the real situation and attack India, they
would be virtually unopposed. If the political situation in India
were to change for the better, this may prevent the enemy from
having any ambitions to enter India.[1]

The Chinese ambassador in London was asked to acquaint
Cripps (who had visited Chiang early in 1940) of this opinion
and to leave Cripps to relay it to Churchill. The Chinese Foreign
Minister in Washington was to place it before Roosevelt. By
25 February Cripps, Churchill, and Roosevelt would have
known Chiang's views.

   Soon after the fall of Singapore Berle had proposed that 'we
once more take up with the British, preferably through Winant
in London, the necessity of making a statement of policy with
respect to India'.[2] At a Senate Foreign Relations Committee
meeting on 25 February there appeared a serious under-
current of anti-British feeling:

Concerning India, the argument was that we are participating on
such a large scale and had done so much for England in Lend-Lease
that we had now arrived at a position of importance to justify our
participation in Empire councils and such as to authorize us to
require England to make adjustments of a political nature within
the framework of her Empire. We should demand that India be
given a status of autonomy. The only way to get the people of India
to fight was to get them to fight for India.[3]

[1] Chiang to T. V. Soong, 24 Feb. 1942, FRUS, 1942, i. 605.
[2] Berle to Welles, 17 Feb. 1942, ibid. 602–4.
[3] Memo. by Asst. Sec. of State to Welles, 25 Feb. 1942, ibid. 606–7.

The Master Lend–Lease Agreement had been signed two days previously. At midnight on the 25th Roosevelt cabled to Winant that he was 'somewhat concerned over the situation in India especially in view of the possibility of the necessity of a slow retirement through Burma to India itself'.[1] He asked Winant or Averell Harriman, the President's Special Representative in London, to deal with all matters relating to Lend–Lease, for 'a slant on what the Prime Minister thinks about new relationships between Britain and India'.

On the morning of the 26th Harriman delivered 'a highly sensitive personal message from Roosevelt inquiring what steps Churchill proposed by way of conciliating the Indian leadership'.[2] He learned of 'the status of the political discussions now going on in London and in India for immediate action and for the future.'[3] Churchill would cable Roosevelt personally after the Cabinet and the Government of India had been consulted.

The War Cabinet's India Committee, which first met on the evening of 26 February, was chaired by Attlee and comprised Amery, Cripps, and Anderson, from the War Cabinet, and Simon and Sir James Grigg, Secretary of State for War and a former Finance Member of the Viceroy's executive. It was charged with preparing a statement to clarify 'beyond any doubt the nature of what we promised to India' and to indicate 'whether any further Constitutional advance should be made at the present time'.[4] The meeting accepted Amery's proposal that some provinces might opt out of the constitutional scheme eventually adopted without retarding the freedom of others.

At its second meeting, at 5 p.m. the following evening, the Committee considered a memorandum by Amery covering a draft Declaration. Taken together the two documents explained that Britain's aim was *full* Dominion status, that Britain would accept an Indian-devised constitution, that failure of the Indian parties to agree should not delay constitutional progress, and that Britain's interests and obligations would be dealt with

[1] Ibid. 604.

[2] W. A. Harriman and E. Abel, *Special Envoy to Churchill and Stalin* (New York, 1975), 129.

[3] Harriman to Roosevelt, 26 Feb. 1942, FRUS, 1942, i. 608.

[4] C.M., 185.

apart from the constitution. As for the present, Amery circulated some notes on alternative possibilities and plumped for the half-way house that he had adumbrated the previous week. Without adopting Amery's draft Declaration the Committee proceeded to agreement upon principles. The document should be short, simple, and explicit. It should be published in Parliament and broadcast to India by the Prime Minister. It would prescribe the procedure for setting up the post-war constituent body, which would consist of provincial assemblies' and states' representatives. Provinces and states would have the right to stand out of the new union. Britain's interests and obligations would be met by a treaty. The constitution would be enacted forthwith by His Majesty's Government. The new Dominion would be free to remain in or separate from the Commonwealth. If the Declaration were accepted in India then Britain would consult Indian leaders on the best way in which they could reinforce the war effort. Amery undertook to embody these principles in a draft for consideration at eleven o'clock next morning.[1]

(iii) Cripps Intervenes

At 10.15 that night, 27 February, Miss Harrison received a telephone call from Lady Cripps, asking her to come to Cripps's flat. When she arrived forty-five minutes later she found Cripps and Geoffrey Wilson poring over Cripps's own draft embodiment of the Cabinet Committee's resolutions. Cripps explained that there would be no further discussions the next day but that the Committee had agreed upon the substance of a Declaration. The Prime Minister had not been at the meeting but would 'stand responsible for whatever is agreed on by this Committee'.[2] He had not seen the statement but 'wanted the thing settled and would agree'. Miss Harrison read the draft while Cripps paced up and down the room.

Miss Harrison had no serious misgivings about the proposed arrangements for the future. Cripps explained that within the Dominion status framework of the new constitution India could

---

[1] India Committee Meeting, 27 Feb. 1942, C.M., 191.

[2] Harrison to Heath, Alexander, and A. Wilson, 28 Feb. 1942, I.C.G., Cripps file.

secede, if it wished, within twenty-four hours. He admitted the danger of Pakistan but argued that 'even Gandhi had said this idea should be among the schemes an Assembly should discuss'. Again, 'if it was admitted as a right—then Congress would go all out to see there was accommodation'.

However, she was highly critical of the statement as an initiative to enlist India's co-operation. She commented:

That though the idea of a Constituent Assembly was accepted and Dominion Status assured—I felt the *present* was what mattered and the desire for control *now*. The future was so problematic—the immediate present was in the forefront of their minds. That this statement—though it certainly made clear the future—did not take sufficient account of great forces unused—and anxious to be used. This could not be ignored. I asked whether the risk of giving power should not be taken; there were wise people who see the trend of events; no one would be foolish enough to sack the Commander-in-Chief etc., they wanted to be associated in great decisions.

Cripps insisted that this was as much as could be got. It 'went just as far as was humanly possible; to get this there had been *enormous* struggles'. He said clearly that 'they could not hand over Defence and foreign affairs; he doubted whether he himself would do so. For it might well be that an Indian Council would demand the recall of the troops in Libya and Burma, etc.—and he could not see the possibility of Home Affairs being taken from Maxwell. In any case—the point was settled and final.' All that could be done to answer Miss Harrison's criticism was to redraft the statement's final paragraph, on the present arrangements, to give 'a really warm feeling of wanting to co-operate in finding together a way out over this transitional period'. In particular, the last sentence was made more forthcoming.

Cripps did say that the Viceroy would have to be recalled and that he was working for this to be inserted in the short statement. Linlithgow was being very obstructive and his recall would be 'an earnest of our intentions that we mean a new deal'.

After a 'memorable two hours' Miss Harrison emerged 'conscious of being a pint measure in the face of an ocean'. It had been 'no light thing to be faced with [Cripps's] brilliant mind', capable of getting 'the guts of a complicated document in three minutes'. But she knew she had 'something he had not got, through all these years of our work—a sense of the minds of the men to whom this statement was going'. To offer India assured post-war Dominion status was 'a great step forward for this stupid country to take too late—but Gandhi and Nehru, Sapru and Jinnah, are facing what may be a panic-stricken multitude and wanting power to deal with it'. If Indians were to be held responsible they would want commensurate authority. It was an ominous assessment.

At its meeting on the 28th the India Committee considered the draft statements that Amery and Cripps had prepared. Cripps's draft is not available for scrutiny, but it seems likely that it contributed more than Amery's to the form and substance of the document that the Committee approved. On 1 March Churchill recorded that he was favourably impressed by the draft. He arranged for it to be brought before the War Cabinet on 3 March and thereafter, 'in consequence of the gravity of the decision' and so as not to 'run the risk of a schism', he wanted all ministers of Cabinet rank to be consulted.[1]

There were drafting changes to the statement between 28 February and 3 March. Amery looked to Churchill and Simon to counteract the more radical inclinations of Cripps and Attlee. On 2 March he appealed to Churchill:

I trust you will support me against being rushed by Cripps and Attlee on either the wording or the date of the declaration. The whole future of India is at stake. Whatever his failings as a stylist or as a negotiator with Indians Linlithgow knows what he is dealing with, has served the Empire faithfully, and is at least entitled to have his views carefully considered. . . . I think Linlithgow may well feel in any case that he is being unfairly rushed and I should not be altogether surprised if he talks of resignation. Cripps and Attlee are very eager to secure this anyhow, and there may be much to be said for a new man to carry out a new policy. . . . In any case we must first see if there is any response to our declaration. We should look silly if we pushed out the Viceroy for lack of enthusiasm about our policy and then found that lack of enthusiasm equally shared by India![2]

[1] Minute by Churchill, 1 Mar. 1942, C.M., 199.
[2] C.M., 206.

Cripps's attempt to have an announcement of Linlithgow's replacement included in the Declaration had failed, though a favourable Congress response to the new policy might well enable him to displace him in the end.

The draft Declaration was placed before the War Cabinet on 3 March. In the light of its suggestion for some relatively small amendments the India Committee that night produced the following, almost final, revise:

Draft Declaration

His Majesty's Government, having considered the anxieties expressed in this country and in India as to the fulfilment of the promises made in regard to the future of India, have decided to lay down in precise and clear terms the steps which they propose shall be taken for the earliest possible realisation of self-government in India. The object is the creation of a new Indian Union which shall constitute a Dominion, associated with the United Kingdom and the other Dominions by a common allegiance to the Crown, but equal to them in every respect, in no way subordinate in any aspect of its domestic or external affairs, and free to remain in or to separate itself from the equal partnership of the British Commonwealth of Nations.

His Majesty's Government therefore make the following declaration:

(a) Immediately upon the cessation of hostilities, steps shall be taken to set up in India, in the manner described hereafter, an elected body charged with the task of framing a new Constitution for India.

(b) Provision shall be made, as set out below, for the participation of the Indian States in the Constitution-making body.

(c) His Majesty's Government undertake to accept and implement forthwith the Constitution so framed subject only to:

  (i) the right of any Province of British India that is not prepared to accept the new Constitution to retain for the time being its present constitutional position, provision being made for its subsequent accession if it so decides.

With such non-acceding Provinces, should they so desire, His Majesty's Government will be prepared to agree upon a new Constitution on lines analogous to those here laid down.

  (ii) the signing of a treaty which shall be negotiated between His

Majesty's Government and the constitution-making body covering all necessary matters relating to the complete transfer of responsibility from British to Indian hands.

Whether or not an Indian State elects to adhere to the Constitution, it will be necessary to negotiate a revision of its Treaty arrangements so far as this may be required in the new situation.

(d) the constitution-making body shall be composed as follows, unless the leaders of Indian opinion in the principal communities agree upon some other form before the end of hostilities:

Immediately upon the result being known of the Provincial Elections which will be necessary at the end of hostilities, the entire membership of the Lower Houses of the Provincial Legislatures shall, as a single electoral college, proceed to the election of the constitution-making body by the system of proportional representation. This new body shall be in number about one-tenth of the number of the electoral college.

Indian States shall be invited to appoint representatives in the same proportion to their total population as in the case of the representatives of British India as a whole, and with the same powers as the British Indian members.

(e) While during the critical period which now faces India, and until the new Constitution can be framed, His Majesty's Government must inevitably bear the full responsibility for India's defence, they desire and invite the immediate and effective participation of the leaders of the principal sections of the Indian people in the counsels of their country, to give their active and constructive help in the discharge of a task so vital and essential for the future freedom of India.[1]

In particular, the War Cabinet had asked 'whether paragraph (e) . . . should be made more explicit, and if not, what answer should be given when we were asked in what way we hoped that the leaders of the principal sections of the Indian people would participate in the counsels of their country'.[2] Paragraph (e) was almost certainly Cripps's work, incorporating the 'more forthcoming' emphasis that Miss Harrison had suggested. It was now vaguer than in Amery's superseded draft of 28 February, which stated that the immediate changes would be within the existing framework of the con-

[1] C.M., 229.
[2] War Cabinet Conclusions, 3 Mar. 1942, C.M., 222 .

stitution.[1] In his 2 March appeals for Churchill's help Amery advised that the paragraph 'may want strengthening' in order to exclude the possibility of a Sapru-type national government responsible to the Crown.[2] Linlithgow, too, had indicated his expectation that the paragraph might lead him to the position that his 'utmost limit' proposals of 25 February contemplated, and wished 'to know whether . . . [they were] an acceptable presentation of the hand to be played'.[3]

The India Committee agreed to meet the point by drafting instructions to the Viceroy, and it approved the following text that Cripps prepared:

You are authorized to negotiate with the leaders of the principal sections of Indian opinion, upon the basis of paragraph (e) of the declaration, for the purpose of obtaining their immediate support for some scheme by which they can partake in an advisory or consultative manner in the counsels of their country.

This does not preclude you offering them—if you consider it wise or necessary—positions in your executive council, provided this does not embarrass you in the defence and good government of the country during the present critical time.[4]

The draft was consistent with the opinion of Mr. H. W. Emerson, a former Home Member of the Government of India and Governor of the Punjab (1933–8), which, together with the War Cabinet's question, the Committee had before it. Emerson advised going beyond paragraph (e) to give 'an immediate earnest of British intentions'.[5] Subject to 'the Viceroy keeping effective control over the safety of India and internal order, and the Commander-in-Chief retaining his responsibility for defence', he saw no objection to 'reconstituting the Viceroy's Executive Council, adding a Defence Minister, and bringing in representatives of the Congress and the Muslim League'.

On 4 March Churchill acquainted Roosevelt that a declaration of post-war Dominion status carrying the right of secession was under consideration. The same day the War Cabinet agreed to the circulation of the draft to all Cabinet ministers, who should be invited to meet the next day.

[1] C.M., 193.   [2] C.M., 206.
[3] Linlithgow to Amery, 2 Mar. 1942, C.M., 209.
[4] India Committee, 3 Mar. 1942, C.M., 223.
[5] Note by Emerson, 3 Mar. 1942, C.M., 221.

At noon on Thursday 5 March, in his room at the House of Commons, Churchill presented the Declaration to ministers 'with a bias against'.[1] The meeting is not officially recorded, but Sir Alexander Cadogan noted that it precipitated talk of resignations from the War Cabinet. A letter that Amery wrote to Churchill sums up the significance of the meeting:

The one thing that stands out from this morning's meeting is that the declaration will be damned by everybody if it is issued without the *fullest accompanying explanation* of what is the deadlock we are trying to solve and so to bring Indians into cooperation now, what we mean to insist upon in the Treaty, etc. etc. It was quite clear to me that hardly any one who spoke had really grasped what the declaration is driving at. . . . On that basis of full explanation the thing can go through and will satisfy Moslems and *just possibly* some of Congress, as well as Americans and Left Wing here. But we shall have to think again very carefully before proclaiming to the world and the Indian soldier that India can walk out of the Empire.[2]

R. A. Butler told Hoare that the meeting had put paid to the Declaration: 'The Indian scene has come to the front. We had a great meeting of all members of the Government. . . . The Conservative reaction, i.e. the view that some British interest must be retained in India, appears to be on top of any other influence. There will therefore not be a statement in the immediate future, and, when it comes, it should not sell everything away.'[3]

On Friday the 6th there arrived a battery of cables from India that represented an assault on the Declaration from a different point of view. The Commander-in-Chief, Sir Archibald Wavell, and the Governor of the Punjab, Sir Bertrand Glancy, were apprehensive of the effect that the local option provision would have upon the Punjab and its considerable contribution to the war effort. The Muslim majority in the Punjab would favour non-accession but would become apprehensive of the danger posed by the martial Sikh minority. The Sikhs would feel that Britain was repudiating its pledge to protect the interests of the minorities. Communalism would

---

[1] Dilks, *Cadogan Diaries*, 5 Mar. 1942, 440.

[2] Amery to Churchill, 5 Mar. 1942, C.M., 240.

[3] Butler to Hoare, 6 Mar. 1942, Templewood Papers, University Library, Cambridge, XIII. 19.

at once appear in the armed services, so largely supplied
by the Punjab, with disastrous results. Linlithgow counselled
that if local option was regarded as essential to the Declaration then the best palliative was to reassert the minorities
pledge in it. Even so, the recognition of a Dominion's freedom
to secede would still exacerbate 'minor' minorities' fears, for the
reassuring links with the Crown might be severed summarily.[1]

In London, too, a meeting of Commonwealth High Com-
missioners took exception to the wording in the Declaration
that implied a constitutional right to secede. On the Friday
night, therefore, Amery cabled to Linlithgow: 'Health of
declaration precarious too early yet to say whether moribund.
Phrase explicitly admitting secession will almost certainly be
modified or drop out.'[2] Cadogan noted that the crisis over
India was 'still acute: P.M. will probably have to give way
(otherwise I think Cripps' resignation at stake)'.[3]

After the stormy meeting of ministers on the Thursday the
War Cabinet had assembled and charged the India Committee
with considering the objections raised and reporting back to a
special War Cabinet meeting the following Monday (9 March).
The Committee meeting was set down for the Saturday morning. With the fate of the Declaration in the balance, Amery's
letter to Churchill on the Thursday revived the idea of sending
out an emissary to seek Indian co-operation on the basis of
a general understanding about the future. If the visit succeeded
then the Declaration could be published as a real charter for
India's future. If not the world would realize that no advance
was possible. Amery proposed going to India himself, for to
send anyone else would be 'a slap in the face for Linlithgow'.[4]
On the Friday Butler was aware of vague talk about sending
an emissary to negotiate.[5]

The special War Cabinet meeting was brought forward from
the Monday to 10.30 on the morning of Saturday the 7th.
The India Committee gathered for a brief half-hour before the
meeting. It considered the criticism of the Declaration's

[1] Linlithgow to Amery, 6 Mar. 1942, C.M., 246, 248; Glancy to Linlithgow,
4 Mar. 1942, C.M., 236.
[2] C.M., 249.
[3] Dilks, *Cadogan Diaries*, 6 Mar. 1942, 440.
[4] Amery to Churchill, 5 Mar. 1942, C.M., 240.
[5] Butler to Hoare, 6 Mar. 1942, loc. cit.

opening paragraph on secession from the Commonwealth. Cripps proposed expunging the offending words and inserting in paragraph (c) (*ii*), concerning the treaty, the passage: 'Such treaty will not preclude the Indian Union from a right of secession from the British Commonwealth of Nations, and shall provide for suitable safeguards of all those minority rights as to which undertakings have been given by His Majesty's Government.'[1] Discussion was deferred until later that day. At the War Cabinet the prospects for any immediate Declaration receded still further. The previous evening Linlithgow had cabled tersely to ask for the whole Cabinet to be reminded of his January advice to do nothing and be told that he was 'not . . . in favour of proposed declaration at this time'.[2] Moreover, the morning newspapers had reported a speech of Nehru's to the effect that any promise of post-war reforms was mere quibbling, and that a provisional national government responsible to the people of India should be formed at once. The meeting considered the possibility of soundings being taken in India prior to the issue of the Declaration but reached no conclusion. The India Committee was asked to continue with its revision of the draft as a Declaration of policy, without regard for the occasion of its release. The revise would be placed before the War Cabinet on the Monday and a full meeting of ministers on the Tuesday.

The India Committee reconvened on Saturday afternoon. Of its several amendments to the draft the most important was the adoption, in different words, of Cripps's solution to the problems of secession and the minor minorities. The treaty would 'make provision, in accordance with the undertakings given by His Majesty's Government, for the protection of racial and religious minorities; but will not impose any restriction on the power of the Indian Union to decide in the future its relationship to the other. Member States of the British Commonwealth'.[3] The revise was sent to Linlithgow for his urgent opinion. Before he received it he had turned against local option. He cabled: 'Further reflection and advice has absolutely convinced me that in face of Commander-in-

---

[1] C.M., 262.
[2] Linlithgow to Amery, 6 Mar. 1942, C.M., 250.
[3] C.M., 264.

Chief's views I could not possibly stand for a declaration containing local option in this form.'[1] The cable crossed Amery's brief intimation, dispatched after the India Committee meeting, that the Declaration was unlikely to be announced, but that a simplified declaration might issue later in the week.[2]

There was also opposition among ministers and at the India Office against local option. After the meeting of ministers on the 5th Butler had written to Hoare: '. . . it would appear that the powers-that-be are reconciled to the idea of a Moslem Confederation in the North. This means two Indias, and I am pressing for some form of central government.'[3] He appealed to Amery. The impression created by the Declaration was that 'the unity of India—the goal of British policy hitherto—must be set aside'.[4] The opting out of Muslim provinces was certain, yet no provision was made for any central government to link them with the acceding provinces. Similarly, the Secretary of State's Advisers criticized local option as opening 'unnecessarily wide the door leading to the disintegration of India'.[5]

On the Saturday Churchill acquainted Roosevelt of the anxiety in India about the effect of local option on the war effort. He summed up the difficulty that the Declaration was presenting: 'We are still persevering to find some conciliatory and inspiring process, but I have to be careful that we do not disturb British politics at a moment when things are increasingly aquiver.'[6]

On the Sunday, at Chequers, Cripps came to the rescue—of the Declaration, the War Cabinet, and, ironically, of Linlithgow. He set down the draft of a statement to the effect that 'His Majesty's Government has decided to send immediately to India a Member of the War Cabinet with full power to discuss with the leaders of Indian opinion the scheme upon which the War Cabinet has agreed, with a view to seeing whether it meets with that generous measure of acceptance which would be vital to its success.'[7] Cripps offered to make the visit himself.

[1] Linlithgow to Amery, 7 Mar. 1942, C.M., 270.
[2] Amery to Linlithgow, 7 Mar. 1942, C.M., 266.
[3] Butler to Hoare, 6 Mar. 1942, loc. cit.
[4] Butler to Amery, 6 Mar. 1942, C.M., 255.
[5] Note by Advisers to Sec. of State, 6 Mar. 1942, C.M., 254.
[6] Churchill to Roosevelt, 7 Mar. 1942, C.M., 271.
[7] Note by Cripps, 8 Mar. 1942, C.M., 281.

His intervention was accepted with alacrity by Churchill and, on the Monday, by the War Cabinet.

The War Cabinet's acceptance of Cripps's offer to take the Committee's revised Declaration to India was accomplished only hours before Linlithgow's intention to resign arrived. His hostile response to the revise, though received before the War Cabinet's noon meeting, was not considered. It may have been suppressed in the interests of unity. He repeated that Wavell regarded the Declaration as disastrous, and added that, in his own view, it was a calamity.[1] Only an hour or so after the War Cabinet meeting Amery received a further cable in which Linlithgow stated that he proposed 'immediately before the announcement is made to telegraph to Winston my resignation'.[2]

Churchill replied to Linlithgow himself:

Yesterday before I was shown your [cable] we decided not to publish any declaration now but to send a War Cabinet Minister out to see whether it could be put across on the spot. . . . The announcement of [Cripps's] mission will still febrile agitation. . . . Do not . . . think of quitting your post at this juncture, for this might be the signal for a general collapse in British Indian resistance with serious rupture of political unity here. We have a very bad time immediately ahead but nothing like so bad as what we have already forced our way through.[3]

Amery was more explicit: '. . . your going at this moment would have precipitated the whole question of policy into acute party conflict and might well have broken up the Government here'.[4] The meeting of ministers was greatly relieved by the dropping of the Declaration, for they were made aware not only of the Wavell and Linlithgow objections to it, but also the threat of resignation with which they would have been faced.[5]

The Declaration, now to become famous as the Cripps offer, was a large advance in British constitutional policy. It guaranteed India the freedom immediately after the war to make its own constitution in the form of dominionhood or independence.

[1] Linlithgow to Amery, 9 Mar. 1942, C.M., 284.
[2] Linlithgow to Amery, 9 Mar. 1942, C.M., 290.
[3] Churchill to Linlithgow, 10 Mar. 1942, C.M., 294.
[4] Amery to Linlithgow, 10 Mar. 1942, C.M., 304.
[5] Amery to Linlithgow, 10 Mar. 1942, C.M., 303.

This was a sharp break with past assumptions of India's subordination within the Empire, even as a Dominion. Provinces dissenting from the constitution might achieve their freedom separately. The need for such a settlement of the provinces' constitutional rights was indicated by Cripps's discussions with the Muslim leaders in December 1939, and the August 1940 offer had assured the Muslims that they would not be coerced into a Hindu-dominated dominion. The right of the princes to stand out of the post-war Union of India was a further break with the no-freedom-without-unity policy. The provision for a treaty, whereby Britain would discharge her obligations to the dissident states and the minorities, set a time limit for the final transfer of power.

This sharp departure in policy was the consequence of the overthrow of the formerly dominant Conservative influence in the War Cabinet. Wartime defeats and dependence upon the U.S.A. abroad and the Labour Party at home made the pressures for change irresistible.

In these circumstances Cripps became confident that Linlithgow could be displaced by a new Viceroy who would bring Congress and the League together in a reconstructed executive, acting as a national government. He accepted as impracticable in wartime a constitutional change in the status of the executive. The Viceroy must have overriding powers to ensure internal order and unity of the military command. Nevertheless, given Britain's intention to quit after the war, there seemed every reason to expect that the Viceroy and his council would normally agree upon wartime policies. Cripps got everything that he wanted into the Declaration, except the replacement of Linlithgow, which must depend upon the Indian parties' response. By 3 March the War Cabinet had accepted his draft instructions empowering the Viceroy to reconstruct his council.

To Cripps's dismay, the new policy was called in question when Churchill presented it to the full, essentially Conservative, Cabinet on Thursday 5 March. Events had moved too fast for ministers to digest the change at once. It was offensive to some that India was to be told that it might walk out of the Empire. To others it seemed that the unity of India was being wilfully shattered. Such Cabinet dissidents would be strengthened by

Linlithgow's opposition to the Declaration. Broadly speaking, during the crucial days of 5–8 March there was a Cripps–Labour axis for making the Declaration and a Conservative–Linlithgow one against. Churchill, Amery, and their Conservative War Cabinet colleagues were opposed to the change on principle but had been forced of necessity to yield ground.

Had Cripps stood firm that week-end a crisis would have arisen on the Monday when Linlithgow's resignation arrived. He regained the initiative and averted the loss or erosion of the Declaration by offering himself as' emissary. He hoped that, given the negotiating powers that he had drafted for the Viceroy, he would secure Indian co-operation, proclaim the Declaration, and thereby dispose of Linlithgow. But he had also saved the Churchill government, enabled Churchill to reject Linlithgow's resignation, and, by removing himself from the London scene, enabled his adversaries to recover their ascendance in the India Committee and the War Cabinet. Lacking strong support at home he needed to win over the Congress; yet by seeking the agreement of the very party the Tories most mistrusted he risked being repudiated by his own government.

4

THE SECOND VISIT
(March–April 1942)

(i) Cripps's Powers

WHEN CRIPPS set off for India on Saturday 14 March he had no specific instructions from the War Cabinet save those, suitably rephrased by the India Committee at the War Cabinet's request, that he had himself drafted on 3 March as appropriate instructions for the Viceroy. The only significant drafting change was the expression of an expectation that, with regard to the provision that the reconstruction of the executive should not embarrass defence or good government, he would 'no doubt consult with the Viceroy and Commander-in-Chief, and will bear in mind the supreme importance of the military situation'.[1] In the announcement of the mission that he drafted on 8 March Cripps had referred to an emissary with 'full power to discuss with the leaders of Indian opinion the scheme upon which the War Cabinet has agreed'.[2] If they accepted the scheme His Majesty's Government would announce their decisions and call them into immediate consultation.

Both Cripps's instructions and his draft announcement went further than Churchill's announcement of the mission before Parliament on 11 March. Churchill said only that Cripps would strive to procure the Indian parties' *assent* to the Declaration, with a view to the Declaration promoting the 'concentration of all Indian thought upon the defence of the native soil'.[3] He would also consult with the Viceroy and the Commander-in-Chief on the military situation, bearing in mind His Majesty's

[1] India Committee, 9 Mar. 1942, C.M., 283.
[2] Cripps's Note, 8 Mar. 1942, C.M., 281.
[3] C.M., 308.

Government's paramount responsibility for India during the war.

Yet it was logical and necessary that Cripps should 'negotiate ... some scheme' for the reconstruction of the executive, for the Indian leaders could hardly accept the Declaration unless the meaning of paragraph (e), that is to say, the means of their participating in the counsels of their country, were clear.

Cripps's instructions unquestionably authorized him to negotiate the membership of the Viceroy's council: 'You may offer them, if you consider it wise or necessary, positions in the Executive Council. ...'[1] Churchill was therefore misleading when he advised Linlithgow to await Cripps's arrival: 'He is of course bound by the draft declaration which is our utmost limit.'[2] Cripps's powers were larger than the Declaration indicated. He was indeed to consult the Viceroy and the Commander-in-Chief but was not bound by their opinions, only by the criteria of sound defence and good government. The only constraint imposed by the Declaration's paragraph (e) was the reservation to His Majesty's Government of the full responsibility for India's defence. The limit imposed by Cripps's instructions was that the scheme for the executive must be no more than advisory or consultative. The constitutional implication of Cripps's brief was that Cripps might contemplate the minor change of waiving the requirement for three official members of the executive, but might not negotiate away the Viceroy's statutory power to discharge his special responsibilities.

The brief was wider than some members of the War Cabinet intended or understood. When the War Cabinet approved the mission on 9 March it attached importance to the announcement 'making it clear that the Lord Privy Seal was taking out to India a specific scheme approved by the War Cabinet. Otherwise, it would be said that he was going out to negotiate.'[3] The India Committee's instructions to Cripps, which were finalized at a meeting on the afternoon of Monday 9 March, seem not to have been referred back to the War Cabinet. But they were read out to the meeting of ministers the next day.

[1] C.M., 283.
[2] Churchill to Linlithgow, 10 Mar. 1942, C.M., 294.
[3] War Cabinet, 9 Mar. 1942, C.M., 282.

Amery's glosses on Cripps's brief indicate a vagueness about the limits of Cripps's powers. On 9 March he wrote to Churchill:

While it is essential that Sir S. Cripps should work to a definite set of instructions, and that there should be no idea that he is going out on a purely roving commission, I think there are serious objections to referring to his instructions as if they were an absolutely cut and dried plan (even though from our point of view they are something fairly near that). To do so seems to me to fetter the Cabinet's emissary's discretion too much.[1]

His proposed wording of Churchill's announcement of the mission stated that Cripps went furnished with instructions approved by the War Cabinet to discuss the Indian deadlock with the Viceroy and the Indian leaders. His words were lost in Churchill's own draft. Amery advised Linlithgow that Cripps was going out to endeavour to see if he could by negotiation with Indian political leaders secure agreement upon the Declaration: 'Cabinet definitely want him to treat their draft as the basis of his instructions. . . . His instructions will . . . be to keep in closest touch with you and Commander-in-Chief from point of view of not embarrassing military situation.'[2] Cripps's task was 'squaring the circle'.[3] Amery told Linlithgow that the War Cabinet was prepared to bring in political leaders in some form or other without surrendering control of the executive for war purposes.[4] Cripps was to go and discuss and negotiate to see how far Indians would accept the Declaration.[5] On 12 March he cabled that on the immediate problem of securing full Indian co-operation in the war effort Cripps would 'consult with you'.[6]

It is a fair generalization that while Cripps was bound absolutely by the long-term policy of the Declaration, in the short-term Churchill and Amery expected him to reach agreement with Linlithgow on a reconstitution of the executive that the Indian leaders would accept. Of the India Committee Simon, Anderson, and Grigg probably had a similar expectation. On the other hand, Attlee and Cripps had long been critical of Linlithgow. From their point of view the need for the mission was evidence of his failure to bring the parties together to

[1] C.M., 291. [2] 10 Mar. 1942, C.M., 296.
[3] Ibid. [4] C.M., 302.
[5] Amery to Linlithgow, 10 Mar. 1942, C.M., 304. [6] C.M., 315.

cooperate with the war effort. In his own draft announcement of the mission Cripps made no reference to discussions with the Viceroy. In literal terms, Cripps was not obliged to convince Linlithgow of the wisdom of his scheme for reconstituting the Viceroy's executive, though he would need to convince the War Cabinet. As emissary he took over the instructions originally intended for the Viceroy on the reconstruction of the executive. If Cripps could secure the Indian parties' broad agreement to enter the executive on an advisory or consultative basis, consistent with good government and sound defence, then it would be for His Majesty's Government to call them into consultation on details.

Cripps's powers were not made clear to Linlithgow. At 6 a.m. on 10 March Amery cabled that Cripps's further general instructions as to the interpretation to be put on paragraph (e) would be sent separately and would 'of course have to be discussed with you in detail'.[1] At 9 p.m. he cabled that on further consideration it seemed more appropriate that these instructions should be 'left for discussion between you on his arrival'.[2] In the interim Cripps and Amery had had a long discussion.[3] It is not known whether Cripps asked for his brief to be kept secret or whether Amery decided that the instructions might provoke Linlithgow to resign after all. Linlithgow later claimed that he was *never* told what instructions the War Cabinet had issued to Cripps. It is the case that, at the request of one of Cripps's staff, the instructions were cabled out *via* the Viceroy on 28 March, five days after Linlithgow's first meeting with Cripps. Of course Linlithgow himself may not have read the cable.

Cripps undoubtedly assumed that he was charged with negotiating with the parties' leaders for the reconstruction of the executive within limits that Linlithgow might feel unable to accept. On 4 April he cabled to Churchill: 'The only point . . . for negotiation is the content of clause (e) which as you know was purposely left vague apart from the general principle of the retention of defence.'[4] After the failure of the mission he told a press conference in London that paragraph (e) was

specially left in what I may call a vague condition, in order that it might allow the greatest area for negotiation. It was only considered

[1] C.M., 295.   [2] C.M., 300.
[3] Amery to Linlithgow, 10 Mar. 1942, C.M., 303.   [4] C.M., 519.

desirable as regards paragraph (e) to make the one reservation as regards defence. The whole of the rest was left open so that the most effective means might be devised and discussed by which the objective of the fullest and most effective participation by the leaders of Indian opinion could take place.[1]

He told his wife that he had 'a private cipher code straight to the Prime Minister' and 'powers if he sees fit to use them'.[2]

Cripps carried with him a sense of mission. He went out as an emissary bearing a scheme agreed by the War Cabinet, but the fact that it was essentially his own scheme, devised and developed over the last four years, made him something of a missionary come to proclaim a new order. Among the characteristics that he shared with Linlithgow were piety and self-importance, so that their conflict of political philosophies was almost certain to produce a point-counterpoint relationship. Professor Sir Reginald Coupland was well placed to appreciate the piquancy of their encounter, for which his diary entries serve to set the stage.

Coupland was staying at Viceroy's House, New Delhi, early in March, after spending some three months in India with a view to writing a report for Nuffield College on the history of the constitutional problem and its possible solution. He was with Linlithgow for about an hour on Monday the 9th, some three hours after Linlithgow had cabled his intended resignation. Linlithgow 'held forth earnestly and fluently, but evidently weighed down by the incapacity of Indians and his war responsibility'.[3] He lamented the 'desperate incapacity of Indians for self-government', their want of 'political instinct or moral courage', and mused, like a Victorian Viceroy, that 'perhaps the natural leaders are the Princes'. Aware of the 'value of uniting India in opposition to Japan', he nevertheless feared the 'risks in any drastic change. . . . The cardinal factor is the Army. Remember the greased cartridges. Suppose India were lost and with it the war.' Coupland summed up:

My general impression was that his intellectual capacity is distinctly greater than I supposed, and his honesty and sense of duty command one's admiration: but his instincts are conservative: he raises all possible objections to any course: he wants to go slowly and

---

[1] Press Conference, 22 Apr. 1942, C.M., 665 (p. 815).
[2] Harrison to Heath, 2 Apr. 1942, I.C.G., Cripps file.
[3] C.D., 9 Mar. 1942.

cautiously with as little risk as possible: he had planned his own time-table of political advance, and didn't like being jolted on. Also a touch of Curzonian self-sufficiency though not arrogance. He seems to feel the *whole* burden rests on him *alone*. I was much moved by his repeated stress on the weight of his responsibility towards the end; and, as I left, I tried stumblingly to express my gratitude as a humble British patriot.

As Cripps invited him to join his team, Coupland stayed on to become, in the words of H. V. Hodson, the Reforms Commissioner of the Government of India, 'the one "independent" witness from the inside of all that happened'.[1] He recorded his first major interview with Cripps on 26 March:

> He . . . walked up and down the room talking in the frankest way on his mission and personal prospects, and the inferences which he hoped his Congress friends would draw. His success would make him the dominant person in Indian policy for 20 years. His failure would leave Indian nationalism without a friend in England of the front rank. He put his desire for Indian freedom first: all personal risk second.[2]

The note suggests what Cripps made plain to Lionel Fielden of the *Observer* that if Cripps could reach agreement with Congress on the reconstruction of the executive then his power would be such as to enable him to overcome any resistance that Linlithgow might offer: 'I told Nehru that if they accepted my terms *I* should be such a Tremendous Figure in England that *I* could do everything.'[3] A. D. K. Owen, a Welsh socialist and a part-time leader writer for *The Times* who had become Cripps's aide in February, went so far as to say that 'if he brought this settlement off, Cripps would certainly replace Winston'.[4] Conversely, Cripps attempted to use the leverage of his personal position by telling Azad, the Congress president, that 'if this scheme was not accepted, they would find that those who had been their best friends in British political circles in the past were no longer able to do anything to assist them towards the aims which they had'.[5]

[1] Hodson to Coupland, 8 May 1942, Appx. I, C.D.
[2] C.D., 26 Mar. 1942.
[3] Fielden to E. Thompson, n.d. [Aug. 1942], quoted in P. S. Gupta, *Imperialism and the British Labour Movement*, 270 n. 225.
[4] C.D., 3 Apr. 1942.
[5] Interview, 28 Mar. 1942, C.M., 416.

Assuredly, Cripps had powers, but unless he could win over Congress Linlithgow would be irremovable and Conservatism would again become a major force in the making of Indian policy at home. Cripps himself would be caught between giant millstones, the dominant parties of Britain and India.

(ii) Towards a Quasi-Cabinet

Cripps arrived at New Delhi airport at about 1 p.m. on Monday 23 March. He was met by the Viceroy and Lieut.-Gen. G. N. Molesworth, representing the Commander-in-Chief. His party included, besides Owen, Mr. F. F. Turnbull, private secretary to the Secretary of State, and Mr. Graham Spry, a Canadian who was Cripps's personal assistant. Together with Coupland they were to be known as 'the Crippery'. Cripps stayed at Viceroy's House until Wednesday the 25th, when he moved to 3 Queen Victoria Road, the house of Sir Andrew Clow, Communications Member of the Viceroy's executive, who was on leave. He was therefore able to conduct his interviews with party and princely representatives quite privately, though he made a practice of visiting Linlithgow each evening after dinner.

At their first private discussion, after lunch on the day of his arrival, Cripps showed Linlithgow a list of a reformed executive, Indian except for the Commander-in-Chief. 'That's my affair,' said Linlithgow, handing it back.[1] 'He insisted', Cripps noted, 'that so far as the transitional stage was concerned the implementation of paragraph (e) should be done by him as Governor-General.'[2] Cripps accepted that while the choice of personnel was a matter for the Viceroy, the ultimate responsibility for the executive lay with His Majesty's Government. At its request, Cripps agreed to read the Declaration to the existing executive on the Tuesday evening. On that occasion he answered a question about paragraph (e) with an intimation that, apart from defence, the participation of Indians in the reconstituted executive 'would be welcome to any extent that His Excellency desired'.[3] Linlithgow cabled Amery for his reaction to the removal of the three official members, and counselling him

---

[1] H. V. Hodson, *The Great Divide: Britain–India–Pakistan* (1969), 98.

[2] Cripps's Note, 23 Mar. 1942, C.M., 368.

[3] Notes on Executive Council Meeting, 24 Mar. 1942, C.M., 377.

against Britain committing itself on the matter, or on the form of the executive, until the parties' responses to the Declaration were known. Amery replied that though the War Cabinet were not committed on the point 'they would be prepared for positions on Executive Council to be offered to political leaders provided this would not embarrass the defence and good government of the war during the present critical time'.[1] He would not say that the War Cabinet would not reduce and abolish the official membership—save the Commander-in-Chief—'if this were presented as essential part of agreement with political leaders but it goes without saying that they would pay particular attention to your and Commander-in-Chief's views on effect this might have on Defence and good government. . . .' Indirectly Amery was acquainting Linlithgow of Cripps's instructions.

Cripps began his meetings with the Indian leaders on Wednesday the 25th. The first to come was Azad, the Congress president, accompanied by his secretary, Asaf Ali, at 3 p.m. Next, at 4.30, was Jinnah.

Despite Linlithgow's opposition Cripps showed Azad his proposal for the new executive. The present members would resign and be replaced by men chosen by the Viceroy from lists of nominees furnished by the Indian parties. The executive would be fully Indianized save for the Commander-in-Chief. 'The system of Government would not, however, be changed.'[2] The Viceroy would function 'as a constitutional head like the King in the United Kingdom', normally accepting the advice of his Council. The Council would approximate to a Cabinet in its operation. Azad misunderstood Cripps, believing him to say that the Viceroy's special responsibilities and veto would be revoked. (Molesworth has claimed that his command of English was limited.) Most of the discussion concerned defence. Cripps gathered that Congress wanted the 'appearance' of a Defence Minister. While Azad accepted that Britain must control strategy and the movement of forces, it was important for Congress to feel that it was free to mobilize 'the forces of the Indian people . . . [in] the defence of their country'.[3]

[1] Amery to Linlithgow, 25 Mar. 1942, C.M., 381.
[2] A. K. Azad, *India Wins Freedom* (Bombay, 1959), 57. Azad dates this meeting incorrectly.
[3] Cripps's Note, 25 Mar. 1942, C.M., 379.

Jinnah had grown in political stature since Cripps had met him at his house on Malabar Hill in December 1939. With the avowed goal of sovereign Muslim homelands, he was increasingly accepted as the spokesman for Muslim nationhood. In June 1940 the League had resolved that he alone should control negotiations with the Viceroy and that no League member should serve on any war committee without his consent. In July 1941 he was able to force the Muslim Premiers of the Punjab, Bengal, and Assam to resign from the National Defence Council. His early reception by Cripps bespoke his importance. Cripps explained the change in his own views since 1939, when he had regarded Pakistan as a mere bargaining device. Jinnah now seemed rather surprised that the Declaration went so far to meet the Pakistan case.[1] Cripps was impressed by his attitude. As for the present, he seemed keen 'to mobilize the whole of India behind her own defence', and 'did not seem to think that there would be any insuperable difficulty, provided the Viceroy would consult the Congress and himself on the composition of the Executive and would treat the Executive as a Cabinet rather than as the Executive according to the constitution'.

After the meeting Cripps cabled to ask Churchill's approval for the publication of the Declaration on the following Sunday, 29 March. The step was accepted as necessary not only by the India Committee and the War Cabinet but by Linlithgow and the Governors as well. Once Cripps had acquainted the Viceroy's executive and the Indian leaders of His Majesty's Government's policy it was impossible not to release the Declaration, for it was bound to be leaked. The statement that had, only three weeks earlier, provoked consternation among Cabinet ministers, the Viceroy, the Commander-in-Chief, and the Governor of the Punjab, was now to be released without producing a tremor. The mission had succeeded, in effect, in consolidating the Cripps–Labour policy of post-war freedom, if necessary by partition.

At their meeting on Wednesday night Linlithgow referred Cripps to the cables to Amery and the Cabinet in which he cautioned against offering the Indianization of the executive as part of a political deal with the Indian leaders. However, if Cripps could get both parties to agree to the Declaration he

[1] Cripps's Note, 25 Mar. 1942, C.M., 380.

'was prepared to take big risks because the situation would call for them'.[1] He would 'pay the big price by way of the Executive Council'. If Cripps could 'do the big thing he would not find His Excellency falling short'. But there was a limit: 'His Excellency ... would forgive him almost anything except stealing His Excellency's cheese to bait his own trap.'

The language is obscure and seems to suggest the awkwardness between the two men. Linlithgow was probably offering to effect the full Indianization of his executive if Cripps could win the agreement of both parties to the Declaration, while objecting to Cripps offering full Indianization as a bribe to secure the parties' support. Linlithgow's acting secretary noted that Cripps 'agreed and thought His Excellency's attitude reasonable'. It is impossible that Cripps could have agreed to more than he had conceded to Linlithgow at their Monday meeting: that the choice of individuals was for the Viceroy but the ultimate responsibility for the executive was the British government's. For throughout the afternoon he had been assuring Azad and Jinnah not only that the executive would be Indianized but also that it would become a quasi-Cabinet. Both H. V. Hodson and the journalist Shiva Rao testify that soon after he arrived in Delhi he told them that he intended full Indianization and quasi-Cabinet government.[2]

There is no question of Cripps misleading Linlithgow on the point. On the Sunday that the Declaration was released he explained paragraph (e) to a press conference:

The intention of this paragraph is to indicate to the Governor [-General] who is responsible for the formation of a Government in India, the broad lines upon which, in accordance with the scheme, that Government might be formed. . . . The object of the scheme is to give the fullest measure of government to the Indian people at the present time consistent with the possibilities of a constitution which cannot be changed until the end of the war. . . . You cannot change the constitution. All you can do is to change the conventions of the constitution. You can turn the Executive Council into a Cabinet. . . . The leaders of the principal sections of the Indian people are to be

[1] Memo. of conversation on 25 Mar. 1942, C.M., 384.
[2] Hodson, op. cit., 103; B. Shiva Rao, 'India, 1935–47', C. H. Philips and M. D. Wainwright (eds.), *The Partition of India* (1970), 428; B. Shiva Rao, *India's Freedom Movement: Some Notable Figures* (Delhi, 1972), 160–1.

invited to play their full and effective part which means to say that
the intention of this document is as far as possible subject to the
reservation of defence to put power into the hands of Indian leaders.
. . . We want the Government of India to be fully Indianized.[1]

The Viceroy did not demur at this perfectly precise statement.
Neither did the India Committee or the War Cabinet. It was
not until some days later, when Cripps was considering ways of
conceding to Congress the appearance of a Defence Minister,
that his adversaries could find any ground for cavilling at his
use of his powers in the pursuit of his mission. The assumption of an Indianized quasi-Cabinet runs through Cripps's
further interviews with the Indian leaders.

(iii) Cripps and the Congress

Cripps met Gandhi for about two hours on Friday 27 March.
Gandhi emphasized that he had 'not . . . anything to do with
Congress officially'.[2] He intended to remain in Delhi to attend
a Working Committee meeting the next day and return to
Wardha on Sunday night. Cripps found him antagonistic to
the Declaration, which he expected Congress to reject.[3] Gandhi
objected that the autocratic princely states were to persist under
British protection. Cripps countered that Britain intended that
the creation of a free Indian Union would set up a movement
for democratization in the states and that it would encourage
them to join the Union. Gandhi criticized the virtual invitation
to the Muslims to create Pakistan. Cripps stressed that the
Declaration envisaged Indian unity and that non-accession
would occur only in the event of disagreement in the constitution-making body. With Britain out of the way Indians
themselves ought to be able to agree upon a constitution for
unity. Cripps felt that he made some impression, but he was
discouraged by Gandhi's inability to recall that at Wardha in
1939 they had gone through Cripps's plan together in detail.
    On Saturday 28 March Cripps met the most moderate of
the Congress leaders, Rajagopalachari, who anticipated that

---

[1] Proceedings of Press Conference, 29 Mar. 1942, C.M., 440.
[2] Cripps's Note, 27 Mar. 1942, C.M., 397.
[3] C.D., 27 Mar. 1942.

Congress would dislike the use of the term 'Dominion' and the provision for local option. His own view was that

it was essential that the Indian Leaders should be able to give some clarion call to the Indians which would stimulate them from their present defeatist attitude and it was as part of this argument that he put forward suggestions that something should be done as regards the redrafting of the last paragraph in order to make it clear that the Indian people were asked to defend their own country and that it was not merely the obligation of the British Government, and he associated with this the recommendation that something should be done about an Indian Defence Minister if we hoped to get the consent of Congress to the document.[1]

He favoured accepting the Declaration and felt that if Nehru agreed then they could carry the Working Committee. Rajaji begged Cripps to adjust the final paragraph to meet what he knew would be Nehru's reaction. His appeal echoed the sentiments of the old moderate mediators, Sapru and Jayakar, who, that morning, had urged upon Cripps the control of defence by an Indian.[2]

Cripps and Rajaji agreed upon the following revise of paragraph (e):

During the critical period which now faces India, the peoples of India must take upon themselves the defence of their own country and the task of organizing this defence must fall upon the Government of India; yet His Majesty's Government must inevitably bear the full responsibility for the successful prosecution of the war in India, both for historical reasons and by virtue of the world-wide nature of the war. They desire and invite . . .[3]

The draft was sent to Linlithgow at 1.30 for his consideration.

At 2 p.m. Cripps met Jinnah and gathered that the League Working Committee had accepted the Declaration in principle.[4] Later in the day Sikander Hyat Khan confirmed this news,

[1] Cripps's Note, 28 Mar. 1942, C.M., 412.
[2] Ibid. 411.
[3] C.M., 429.
[4] Cripps's Note, 28 Mar. 1942, C.M., 413. The Central Intelligence Bureau Secret Report (d. 28 March) on the Muslim League Working Committee meeting of 27 March observed that Jinnah was 'prepared to accept the [Cripps] proposals in principle and . . . there was no serious attempt to challenge his judgment' (Home Pol. 221/40).

and argued that in order to win over Congress some appearance
of defence responsibility should be given to an Indian.[1] In the
afternoon, too, Azad again told Cripps of his concern over the
defence portfolio, though he seemed to accept that His Majesty's
Government must control strategy and troop movements.

On Saturday night Cripps and Linlithgow agreed the following wording:

His Majesty's Government must inevitably bear the full responsibility for and retain the ultimate control and direction of the
Defence of India as part of their world war effort, but the task of
organizing to the full the military, moral and material resources
of India must be the responsibility of the Government of India
with the co-operation of the peoples of India.[2]

Cripps cabled this to Churchill, who agreed immediately to
substituting it for the original passage in paragraph (e), save
only for the omission of the words 'full' before 'responsibility'
and 'ultimate' before 'control'.[3] Cripps felt that a real concession had been made to meet the Congress claim.[4]

Nehru arrived in Delhi by train from Allahabad at about
9 a.m. on Sunday 29 March. He had been in bed with fever for
two days and was to remain less than well throughout the
negotiations. Coupland met him at the station and Nehru
joined Cripps for breakfast. Cripps received the impression
that 'the only real difficulty that would emerge would be that
relating to the immediate state of affairs and the allocation of
the Defence Ministry'.[5]

As Nehru had not yet discussed the Declaration with his
colleagues he and Cripps went off to Congress headquarters at
Birla House, where Cripps remained for some three hours.
They were met by Azad, who took them to Gandhi. There
was a good deal of banter, with Cripps trying to pin down
Gandhi to admit that he had approved Cripps's scheme in
December 1939 after a line by line reading of it. Gandhi finally
acquiesced, explaining that he had dismissed the occasion from

[1] Cripps's Note, 28 Mar. 1942, C.M., 417.
[2] Cripps to Churchill, 29 Mar. 1942, C.M., 430.
[3] Churchill to Cripps, 29 Mar. 1942, C.M., 431.
[4] C.D., 28 Mar. 1942.
[5] Cripps's Note, 29 Mar. 1942, C.M., 434.

his mind as merely an encounter with one of the 'globetrotters'.[1]
At Birla House Cripps also met G. B. Pant, a member of the
Working Committee, and B. G. Kher, a member of the A.I.C.C.
Their conversation further confirmed Cripps's impression that
India's association with the defence portfolio was the key to
Congress acceptance of the Declaration.

On Sunday afternoon Nehru and Azad spent almost two
hours with Cripps, who was then able to show them the
approved amendment to paragraph (e). The use of the term
'Dominion', the position of the states, local option, defence, all
were rehearsed. Nehru seemed tired and not well.[2] He was
'very friendly, very receptive, and ... listened to [Cripps's]
arguments without contesting them'.[3] But 'it was so harmonious
as to be almost frightening'. Did this mean, Cripps wondered,
that Congress had already decided upon rejection? Yet Azad
later recalled that Nehru was inclined to consider the proposals
favourably, for all his sympathies lay with the allied cause in the
war.[4] Azad felt that anti-British feeling was so strong in India
that Nehru was unable to state his position emphatically, but
he 'read his unspoken thoughts and sympathised generally with
his views'.

At 6 p.m. on Sunday 29 March Cripps released the Declaration at a press conference in the big circular hall in Lutyens's
Secretariat building. Coupland hailed the occasion as the
Declaration of India's independence. He lauded Cripps's per-
formance as, for two hours, he answered questions from the group
of about one hundred journalists. He 'controlled the conference
superbly—infinitely patient, yet firm, and giving immediate
and frank replies to every question put'.[5] He explained that
the Indian Union would be completely sovereign, free to leave
the Commonwealth at once. While he interpreted paragraph
(e) as offering an Indianized quasi-Cabinet, he was explicit
that 'it would be dishonest to say that the Indian Defence
Minister was responsible for defence'.[6] His Majesty's Government must be responsible for defence, and the Government of

---

[1] C.D., 29 Mar. 1942.
[2] Cripps's Note, 29 Mar. 1942, C.M., 435.
[3] C.D., 29 Mar. 1942.
[4] Azad, *India Wins Freedom*, 59.
[5] C.D., 29 Mar. 1942. See also Coupland, *The Cripps Mission* (1942), 26–7.
[6] Proceedings of Press Conference, 29 Mar. 1942, C.M., 440.

India for organizing India's moral, material, and military forces for defence.

At their meeting that night Cripps told Linlithgow that he knew Gandhi was opposed to the Declaration. Yet he still hoped Congress would find it too difficult to reject. He indicated his intention to force a decision on Wednesday 1 April and leave India by Monday the 6th.

Cripps found Linlithgow willing to discuss the composition of the Council and to appoint an Indian quasi-Defence Minister.[1] Next morning he saw Linlithgow again, to ask whether he might include in a letter to Azad an intimation that the Viceroy was prepared to offer a defence portfolio to an Indian, its functions being those distinguished in paragraph (e) as appropriate to the Government of India. Linlithgow demurred, but agreed to the dispatch of a letter providing for an Indian to be 'connected with the Government of India's Defence responsibilities without in any way impinging upon the functions and duties of the Commander-in-Chief . . . as Supreme Commander . . . or as [Defence] Member of the Executive Council'.[2]

Cripps was cheered by the non-committal reception of the Declaration by Monday morning's newspapers. If Congress had decided on rejection the press would have reflected the fact. During the day it was reported that Gandhi, who had remained in Delhi at Azad's request, had opposed the Declaration as a 'blank cheque on a crashing bank'.[3] In the afternoon Cripps saw Bhulabhai Desai, a member of the Working Committee with whom Cripps had stayed in 1939 and who was 'obviously most anxious to do his utmost to bring about an acceptance of the scheme'.[4] He came essentially to get ammunition for use in the Working Committee.

Nehru dined with Cripps alone on Monday night and they talked late. Cripps had 'never known him more serious and more worried'.[5] Nehru's anxieties gave substance to Gandhi's 'crashing bank' trope. His catalogue of internal disorders and

[1] C.D., 30 Mar. 1942.
[2] Pinnell's Diary, 30 Mar. 1942, C.M., 454.
[3] Ibid. On 31 March Coupland noted that Gandhi was said to have called the Declaration 'a post-dated cheque on a bank which is obviously going broke' (C.D.), which expresses dissatisfaction with the short-term aspect of the offer.
[4] Cripps's Note, 30 Mar. 1942, C.M., 448.
[5] Ibid., 449.

external calamities called in question the possibility of sustaining administrative control and defending India. Refugees from the east were poorly received, unemployment was growing, food was scarce, military collapses in South-east Asia over the past four and a half months were undermining respect for the British in India, and there was growing sympathy for Japan. The situation exacerbated the difficulty of those Congressmen who favoured mobilizing Indian support for the British war effort. Cripps drew the conclusion that while Nehru and Rajaji were 'doing their best to secure acceptance, Gandhi was against it and with his pacifist supporters would probably obtain a majority of the Working Committee'.[1] The great obstacle was 'the non-violence outlook of Gandhi and his supporters on that line, which obviously is opposed to the idea of mobilizing effectively the armed defence of India', rather than 'any particular provision of the scheme itself'.[2]

Before retiring that night Cripps cabled to Amery that while Gandhi was wholly opposed and Rajaji in favour Nehru's attitude would probably be decisive.[3] He regarded the defence question as crucial. He doubted whether the concession made would be sufficient, but could see no compromise that would not 'weaken defence position'.

On the morning of Tuesday the 31st Cripps was 'for the first time taking a dark view of his prospects'.[4] Several of the answers that he gave to questions at a press conference were tinctured with asperity. Nehru had left him despondent about the prospect if his mission failed. 'Lack of food, unemployment, bad transport—everything tends to a popular upheaval. Martial law will fail because there are not enough troops to enforce it. We shan't be able to hold India.' He told Linlithgow that he 'realized that he was finished'.[5] He 'thought Indian leaders had missed an excellent offer, and if anything had to be said on the subject that should be made plain'. Nehru had fought for the scheme but Gandhi 'had made up his mind to prevent the organization of India for war, and was prepared to use any means to thwart it'. Indeed, Cripps imagined Gandhi

[1] C.D., 31 Mar. 1942.
[2] Cripps's Note, 30 Mar. 1942, C.M., 449.
[3] C.M., 458.
[4] C.D., 31 Mar. 1942.
[5] Pinnell's Diary, 31 Mar. 1942, C.M., 459.

to be 'actually desirous to bring about a state of chaos while he sits at Wardha eating vegetables'.[1] He had convinced himself that if he failed it would be because of Gandhi's non-violent creed and his personal power over the Working Committee.

Coupland felt that Cripps viewed the pacifism of the Gandhians on the Working Committee 'from a slightly wrong angle. The "pacifist" majority doesn't refuse co-operation mainly because it would be co-operation in "violent" defence, though this weighs with some of them, but because it would be co-operation with the British, with all its responsibilities, at a time when victory is uncertain.'[2] It is true that in July 1940 and January 1942 the A.I.C.C. endorsed the C.W.C.'s majority decision not to apply Gandhi's non-violence to external defence. A Home Department secret report on the C.W.C. sittings of 30–31 March supports Coupland's contention.[3] It listed several arguments raised against office acceptance, including: that an effective defence against a Japanese invasion was impossible; that Indians would not want to fight the Japanese army because of its Indian National Army element; that a national government could not conclude a separate peace unless it controlled defence; and that Indians would not join the army if defence remained in British hands. Only the last point might be met by a British concession on defence functions. While Azad, Nehru, Rajaji, and Desai sought such a concession in order to win over a C.W.C. majority, such hard-line Gandhians as Patel, Prasad, and Kripalani would still oppose them. Nehru could scarcely have failed to wonder whether, with such opponents, he could form an effective national government, and his reading of the dire circumstances of the country and Britain's reversals must have deepened his pessimism.

Early on the morning of Wednesday 1 April Cripps read to his assembled staff a cable that he proposed sending to Churchill. It predicted the probable rejection of the Declaration, with the defence arrangements the main cause. It told a sombre tale of low morale, anti-British feeling, and administrative dislocation:

. . . if we cannot persuade the Indian leaders to come in now and help us we shall have to resort to suppression which may develop to such a scale that it may well get out of hand. . . . I give you this

[1] C.D., 31 Mar. 1942.　　　[2] Ibid.　　　[3] Home Pol. 221/42.

picture so that you may judge as to the importance from a Defence point of view of getting the Indian leaders into the job of controlling, encouraging and leading the Indian people. This cannot be done under existing circumstances by any Britisher.[1]

He concluded with a request for full authority concerning the duties of an Indian Defence Member, subject to the agreement of the Viceroy and the Commander-in-Chief. However, both Coupland and Linlithgow thought his assessment extreme. And it does seem likely that he had succumbed to Nehru's apprehension of a huge reservoir of civilian discontent, which Gandhi might turn into chaos.

That same morning Cripps abandoned his plan to leave India on Sunday the 5th. Shiva Rao had suggested to him the possibility of reaching a compromise on defence. In consequence, with Linlithgow's agreement he wrote to Azad to invite him, together with Nehru, to meet Wavell and himself in order to discuss the division of defence responsibilities. Wavell was not expected back from a visit to Burma until the week-end.

On the Wednesday afternoon (1 April) Cripps received further hopeful news, from J. C. Gupta, a Bengali Congressman with whom he had stayed in 1939 and a useful link with Birla House.[2] Gupta had learnt from Azad and others that although the C.W.C. objected to much in the scheme

they would not turn it down if they could be satisfied upon the question of Defence; that they felt it was necessary if they were going to take part of the responsibility for rousing India to its own defence that they should be in a position to show the people that they, the people, would exercise some measure of control over Defence.[3]

He said that Gandhi would not prevent acceptance if a majority came out in support of it. He was sure that the Maulana was anxious to arrive at a settlement. When Cripps mentioned his letter to Azad, Gupta went to him to suggest a favourable reply. Soon afterwards Azad's acceptance of the invitation to meet Wavell arrived. Azad added that the C.W.C. had now reached

[1] Cripps to Churchill, 1 Apr. 1942, C.M., 484.
[2] C.D., 1 Apr. 1942.
[3] Cripps's Note, 1 Apr. 1942, C.M., 481.

a decision on the Declaration. When Gupta returned he
intimated to Cripps that the decision amounted to 'only the
Committee's comments on the Declaration and [does] not
close the door to its modification'.[1] Somewhat later Sapru, who
had seen Gandhi, confirmed that further negotiations on defence
might produce a compromise. That evening Cripps cabled to
Churchill his decision to remain until Sunday 12 April in
order to discuss defence with the Congress leaders and Wavell.

On Thursday 2 April Cripps received word from Churchill
that later in the day he would place before the Cabinet his
request to negotiate on defence. He would give no such
authority without the approval of the War Cabinet and the
full Cabinet. Cripps spent part of the morning analysing the
functions of the Defence Department, classifying those essential
to the Commander-in-Chief and those possibly assignable to an
Indian.

At 4.30 Azad and Nehru brought the C.W.C.'s resolution
rejecting the Declaration. It was not to be published and was
susceptible to modification. It rehearsed all the familiar
objections, on the term 'Dominion', local option, the princes,
and defence. It also claimed full responsibility in the Government of India during the war.[2] Cripps was less optimistic after
the meeting than before, but on the strength of Gupta's assurances he thought a settlement still possible if the Defence
Minister question could be agreed.[3]

In London that morning the War Cabinet decided that there
was no reason why some suitable Indian selected by the Viceroy, though not a Congress nominee, should not be appointed
to some office connected with the defence responsibilities of the
Government of India without impairing the Commander-in-
Chief's responsibility for control of the defence of India. It
approved a meeting between the Commander-in-Chief, Cripps,
and the Congress leaders, but the War Cabinet 'must know
what these proposals were, before any commitment was entered
into'. Furthermore, it expressed its unwillingness to consider
any departure from the text of the Declaration.[4]

[1] C.D., 1 Apr. 1942.
[2] Cripps to Churchill, 2 Apr. 1942, C.M., 507.
[3] C.D., 2 Apr. 1942.
[4] War Cabinet, 2 Apr. 1942, C.M., 500.

It is clear that by the time of the War Cabinet meeting on Thursday 2 April Britain's India policy was far less vulnerable than it had been a month earlier. Cripps had succeeded in establishing and publicizing a liberal post-war solution to the Indian problem. The War Cabinet could bask in the warmth with which Cripps's Declaration had been received in the free world. Thus strengthened, Churchill and his colleagues might justly feel that Britain had demonstrated its *bona fides* and that it was now for Congress to reciprocate in the same spirit. Yet Cripps was unable to communicate any change of heart (though the draft rejection from Congress did not reach London until early next morning).

Churchill now decided to stand his ground. He himself under-took to draft a cable to Cripps embodying the War Cabinet's views. It observed that the Declaration had 'made our position plain to the world and . . . won general approval. We all reached an agreement on it before you started and it represents our final position.'[1] It questioned Cripps closely on whether Congress was really prepared to accept, given a solution to the defence question in terms of associating an Indian with certain administrative functions. It repeated the need to consult the full Cabinet on any defence compromise. In the afternoon of the 2nd the India Committee accepted Churchill's draft. That evening the War Cabinet approved its dispatch to Cripps.

(iv) The Linlithgow–Churchill Axis

At its evening meeting on 2 April (Maundy Thursday) the War Cabinet approved another of Churchill's interventions. Linlithgow had cabled to suggest that if there were to be any assignment of defence functions to an Indian both he and Wavell should convey their views to the War Cabinet in their own words. Though their 'relations and mutual understanding [with Cripps] could not be better', it was not possible to express their opinions merely by suggesting amendments or additions to his telegrams.[2] He would 'of course show to Cripps any tele-grams relating to declaration sent to you'. Churchill at once replied encouragingly and the War Cabinet acquiesced. After

---

[1] Churchill to Cripps, 2 Apr. 1942, C.M., 502.
[2] Linlithgow to Amery, 2 Apr. 1942, C.M., 503.

the Cabinet Amery cabled to ask whether Linlithgow's 'personal estimate of present situation or of result of breakdown of present negotiations is as pessimistic as that given by Cripps'.[1] During the Easter week-end, therefore, a direct Linlithgow–Churchill axis emerged from these beginnings, and behind Cripps's back.

Linlithgow replied to the invitation to send a personal estimate:

> I am having an answer prepared but do not feel that I can send it unless I have the Prime Minister's direct and personal instructions to do so. I should find it very difficult to convey my own appreciation of the situation to you in any telegram which, in the absence of instructions to the contrary, I should feel it my duty to show to the Lord Privy Seal.[2]

Churchill replied on Easter Sunday: 'Of course telegraph personal to me or Secretary of State exactly what you think. It is my responsibility to decide to whom it is to be shown after I have read it.'[3] Linlithgow had three documents in draft.[4] The first was his joint opinion with Wavell, accepting as innocuous the appointment of a Defence Co-ordination Member, but emphasizing the need to preserve the Commander-in-Chief's powers as Defence Minister and the constitutional *status quo* in the Viceroy's council. The second was an opinion by Maxwell on Indian morale. The third was an indictment of Cripps's negotiations on the executive, which Linlithgow envisaged using, initially, as an *aide-mémoire* in discussions with Cripps; then, if necessary, as a letter to Cripps; and finally, if further necessary, as a cable home, together with a letter from Wavell on the 'danger of misapprehensions of Cabinet government'. The documents represent Linlithgow's secret armoury for use against Cripps at propitious moments.

Wavell returned to Delhi earlier than expected and Cripps went to see him at noon on Good Friday. He had been to a certain extent forestalled by Linlithgow, who had sent his acting secretary, L. G. Pinnell, to brief Wavell's deputy, General Hartley. Pinnell acquainted Hartley of Cripps's proposed

[1] C.M., 504.
[2] Linlithgow to Amery, 3 Apr. 1942, C.M., 512.
[3] Churchill to Linlithgow, 4 Apr. 1942, C.M., 522.
[4] Pinnell's Diary, 4 Apr. 1942, 43–7, MS. Eur. F125/141, I.O.L.

negotiations on defence and assured him that Linlithgow had
committed himself to 'no weakening, or sharing, or diminution
of the powers and responsibilities of the Commander-in-Chief,
and no modification of the constitutional position'.[1] Linlithgow
was anxious for Hartley to alert Wavell as soon as he returned.
When Cripps saw him Wavell 'refused to have any division in
the Defence Department' but would 'consider a Ministry for
Defence Co-ordination for *liaison* between the Defence and
other Departments'.[2] The meeting with Azad and Nehru was
arranged for 6 p.m. Saturday.

On Good Friday Cripps also drafted his reply to the C.W.C.
resolution. After meeting Wavell he thought he had 'only a
10% chance of agreement'.[3] Coupland recorded a 'general
feeling that little hope remained'. Things seemed less gloomy
on Saturday. Gandhi was finally to leave Delhi that day to
be with his sick wife. He had advised the C.W.C. to follow
Azad. Gupta reported that the Committee was divided: seven
members, including the Gandhians and Nehru, were against
acceptance; five, including Azad and Rajaji, were for, if
satisfaction were achieved on defence. In the latter event
Nehru might also be won over. Among those in favour were
probably Desai, Pant, and Asaf Ali; among those opposed, perhaps Prasad, Patel, Kripalani, Mrs. Naidu, and Sitaramayya.

On Saturday evening Cripps took Azad and Nehru to
Wavell and left them together. No progress was made. Wavell
simply indicated the need for unified control of defence.
Wavell's silences have become celebrated. Cripps observed
later to Agatha Harrison:

Wavell is a most difficult man to talk to. He is very silent, has no
power of drawing out the other person—nor of back and forth
discussion. . . . Until [I] went and brought them together Wavell
had met only Indian *soldiers*—none of the leaders. When Nehru and
Wavell met the latter plainly understood little of what Nehru was
driving at.[4]

Cripps promised to let Nehru and Azad know by Tuesday
morning (7 April) what concession could be offered on defence.

[1] Pinnell's Diary, 2 Apr. 1942, C.M., 510.
[2] C.D., 3 Apr. 1942.
[3] Ibid.
[4] Harrison to Heath and Wilson, 30 Jan. 1945, I.C.G., Cripps file.

Cripps saw Linlithgow and Wavell on the Saturday night and later cabled to Churchill his estimate of the situation. For 'the time has now arrived when a final decision must be arrived at as to how far we are prepared to go on the chance of getting a settlement'.[1] A majority of the C.W.C. might accept the Declaration if the defence offer 'were sufficiently favourable to make any refusal on that ground look ridiculous'. If the offer were accepted there would be no question of Congress seeking a separate peace with Japan. Rejection would mean Britain carrying on the war effort 'in at best a neutral atmosphere and at worst a hostile one'. Suppression would be necessary. There could be no question of taking any defence powers from the Commander-in-Chief *qua* Commander-in-Chief:

18. It is only in his capacity as Defence Minister that any question can arise. Under the new arrangement whereby the Executive Council will approximate to a Cabinet presumably any question coming within the competence of the Government of India as defined in the amended clause (e) will be for decision by the Government of India as a whole and not by any particular Minister.

Cripps was saying that under his assumed quasi-Cabinet government, with collective responsibility, the Defence Minister's functions for mobilizing India's resources for the war might be handled as well by an Indian as by the Commander-in-Chief. He outlined three alternatives: (a) make no concession; (b) transfer the Defence Ministry to an Indian under a written convention that he would not in any matter affecting the prosecution of the war act contrary to the policy laid down by His Majesty's Government and communicated through the Commander-in-Chief; and (c) create a new portfolio for an Indian and transfer to it such matters as the Commander-in-Chief felt he could safely assign. Cripps favoured (b) but would not press it because of Wavell's concern for the confusion it might cause. If the War Cabinet accepted (c) he would propose designating the Commander-in-Chief War Member, converting the Defence Department into the War Department, and creating a Defence Co-ordination Department to take over the transferred functions. He thought Congress unlikely to accept (c), but if they did he proposed to stay in India until the

[1] Cripps to Churchill, 4 Apr. 1942, C.M., 519.

new government was formed. On Easter Sunday, 5 April, the
cable was scrutinized by Linlithgow, Wavell, and Churchill.

Linlithgow sent a pilot telegram to Churchill, intimating
that he and Wavell were still considering their final views.[1]
He agreed to do all that was safe to meet Cripps's wishes on
defence. He did not quarrel with paragraph 18, with its
assumption of quasi-Cabinet government, merely observing
that the Muslims would not want collective responsibility unless
they were in a majority or the Viceroy clearly retained control.
He did demur at the possibility of Cripps remaining to help
reconstitute his executive, which seemed to derogate from his
position.

Churchill's first response was mild too. At 6.30 p.m. on
Sunday he cabled from Chequers (where Lady Cripps was
staying) that Cripps's proposals, together with the views of
Linlithgow and Wavell, would be put to the Cabinet on
Monday evening.[2]

Though Cripps saw Linlithgow on Sunday evening he was
not shown a copy of the pilot telegram. Linlithgow merely said
that he was considering the defence alternatives and favoured
(c). Later, he talked with Wavell, who agreed to send home a
cable in favour of (c), and gave him a copy of the telegram.[3]

Wavell's cable was sent at 5 a.m. Monday.[4] It opposed the
division of the Commander-in-Chief's powers as Commander-
in-Chief and Defence Member but accepted the practicability
of a Defence Co-ordination Member. He 'left it to Viceroy to
safeguard position of . . . [Commander-in-Chief] so that he
cannot be overriden by majority decision in council on essential
matters on defence'.

Once Wavell had sent this opinion Linlithgow released as a
cable the first of the draft documents in his armoury.[5] It was
now put in the form of a reply to Cripps's proposals, but it was
not shown to Cripps before it was sent. It was essentially an
attack upon Cripps's assumption that a reconstituted executive

---

[1] Linlithgow to Amery, 5 Apr. 1942, C.M., 525. Pinnell's Diary, 5 Apr. 1942, 48,
loc. cit.

[2] C.M., 529.

[3] Pinnell's Diary, 5 Apr. 1942, loc. cit.

[4] Wavell to Churchill, 6 Apr. 1942, C.M., 531.

[5] Linlithgow to Amery and Churchill, 6 Apr. 1942, C.M., 530. See n. 4 on
p. 97.

The Linlithgow–Churchill Axis

101

could function as a quasi-Cabinet, and confirmed that both
Linlithgow and Wavell favoured alternative (c) and opposed
transferring the present Defence Ministry to an Indian. In any
event, there could be

no question of majority decisions of the Council being effective
against the requirements of His Majesty's Government .... It is
essential that the position of the Executive Council should not be
glozed over in any clarification of the offer. This is the more necessary because of popular references to an Indian Cabinet or National
Government. The vital test of Cabinet Government, namely,
responsibility to an Indian legislature, does not and cannot exist in
the interim period. The constitutional responsibility of the Governor-
General in Council must remain to Parliament; the Governor-
General must retain his powers of overriding the Executive Council,
and the Secretary of State his powers of direction and control over
the Governor-General in Council. On the other hand non-official
members of the Executive Council appointed for their political influence will always possess in their hands the weapon of resignation.

The Commander-in-Chief must, through the overriding powers
of the Viceroy if necessary, have as much control as required
over the functions of any department that affected the army.

Churchill received these missives from Wavell and Linlithgow in the small hours of Monday the 6th. Thus alerted, at 2.15
a.m. he cabled tersely to Cripps: 'We have not heard anything
here about the words beginning "under the new" down to end
of paragraph. What does this mean?'[1] Coupland had picked up
the point on Good Friday when he had asked Cripps

if it would be clear to Congress that the 'Cabinet' chosen by the
Viceroy in consultation with the political leaders would not be the
same as an ordinary Parliamentary Cabinet since the Viceroy would
have to be free to reject its advice and to dismiss it. I pointed out
that the Viceroy could not divest himself of responsibilities for
Foreign Policy, Minorities, the Princes and the Services. Cripps fully
accepted this. The hope was, he explained, that the V. would
succeed in handling the Cabinet so that a crude conflict of opinion
would not arise.[2]

Cripps's denial of any intention to abrogate the Viceroy's
special responsibilities and veto is wholly consistent with his

[1] Churchill to Cripps, 6 Mar. 1942, C.M., 533.
[2] C.D., 3 Apr. 1943.

disclaimers before the I.C.G. and Miss Harrison in London, and at his 29 March press conference, of any wish to make any such constitutional change or weaken the home government's ultimate control of defence.

Cripps now turned to Linlithgow in the hope that he would be prepared to say that he would attempt to handle a reconstituted executive as if it were a Cabinet. Turnbull suggested to Pinnell that Linlithgow reply to Churchill. The Viceroy's response was 'that this would be rather difficult as we could not reply on this point, and it would be for Sir Stafford Cripps to reply in the light of instructions he had received from H.M.G.'.[1]

When Cripps went to see Linlithgow on Monday morning he was shown the third document in Linlithgow's armoury. It was now in the form of a draft cable to Amery for Churchill. It drew 'pointed attention to the fact that H. E. had all along objected to offering portfolios as a bait for acceptance of a declaration, was uneasy about the loose employment of terms such as "Indian Cabinet" and had been apprehensive of the course of negotiations, but was not aware of what H.M.G.'s instructions were.'[2] Cripps side-stepped confrontation. He could not but agree that Linlithgow's cabled statement of the constitutional position, which he now saw for the first time, was correct. He could object to it only on the grounds that it implied that he was jeopardizing the supremacy of the Viceroy and the British government over the executive. In view of Linlithgow's inflexible and uncooperative posture he would therefore simply cable to corroborate Linlithgow's literal definition of Cabinet government and confirm his own attachment to the constitutional *status quo*. Nevertheless, Linlithgow did not undertake not to send his draft critique of Cripps's negotiations.

On Monday afternoon Linlithgow tried to use an expanded draft of the critique to influence the terms of Cripps's letter, promised for Tuesday morning, on the defence concessions. Cripps was still awaiting the Cabinet's decision on defence, but he had drafted the letter to Azad and showed it to Wavell and Linlithgow.[3] Besides providing for the transfer of defence co-

---

[1] Pinnell's Diary, 6 Apr. 1942, C.M., 539.

[2] Ibid. For the draft see Viceroy to Sec. of State for P.M., secret, Pinnell's Diary, 6 Apr. 1942, 49–51, MS. Eur. F125/141, I.O.L.

[3] C.M., 539; Cripps to Azad, 7 Apr. 1942, C.M., 543.

ordination to an Indian minister, the letter referred to Cabinet
government and envisaged the replacement of the official
members by Indian parties' representatives. Linlithgow argued
that the letter should avoid unnecessary concessions. The letter
was revised in consultation with him and Wavell. 'National
Government' was substituted for the term 'Cabinet government', but Cripps refused to back down over full Indianization,
insisting that the War Cabinet was prepared to eliminate the
official members if necessary.

The War Cabinet's decision arrived overnight. It adopted a
cable that had taken the India Committee two meetings on
Monday to prepare. At the first meeting the Committee had,
in view of Linlithgow's cables, been anxious lest Cripps contemplated a constitutional change in the executive.[1] By its
second meeting Cripps's disclaimer had arrived. Nevertheless
suspicions had been aroused and Cripps was told firmly: 'The
position is and must remain that the Viceroy in Council acts as
a collective body responsible to the Secretary of State and subject to the Viceroy's special powers and duties. . . . There
should be no misunderstanding between you and Indian political leaders on this point.'[2] As for defence, the War Cabinet
agreed to alternative (c), provided the Commander-in-Chief's
authority was not impaired. The India Committee rejected a
proposal by Amery to question whether Cripps intended to
abolish the official members. Cripps was now able to finalize his
letter to Azad. It promised full Indianization, a national government, and the creation of a Defence Co-ordination Minister,
whose functions as agreed by Wavell and Linlithgow were
appended.[3]

Cripps's position was undoubtedly menaced by the emergence
behind his back of a Churchill–Linlithgow axis. Linlithgow,
who had always resented Cripps's quite proper negotiations
over his council, had opened up a direct and secret line of
communication with Churchill, who had never admitted to
himself that Cripps took with him such power to negotiate.
Neither of them had wanted the Cripps–Labour initiative and
both would welcome an opportunity to abort it, especially as it

[1] India Committee, 6 Apr. 1942, C.M., 534.
[2] Draft Cable to Cripps, India Committee, 6 Apr. 1942, C.M., 536.
[3] C.M., 543.

had already enhanced Britain's standing in the eyes of the world.

However, at the very time that Conservatism menaced the mission a countervailing force appeared on the scene—an emissary from a superior power.

(v) The Cripps–Johnson Axis

On Good Friday (3 April) there arrived in Delhi Colonel Louis A. Johnson, the Personal Representative of the President of the United States. He stayed with Linlithgow until Easter Monday, when he moved to a house of his own. Then in his early fifties, his career had been varied, including military service, law, and politics. He had been a member of the West Virginia State Legislature at twenty-six, an aide to the Governor, and the chairman of the House Judiciary Committee. In 1937 Roosevelt had appointed him Assistant Secretary of War.[1]

In December 1941, Bajpai, India's Agent-General to Washington, suggested to Berle of the State Department that the U.S. could help develop India's fighting resources.[2] Berle, in turn, proposed to the Secretary of State that a representative be sent to India to assess its needs in the production of war materials. The idea grew into a plan for a production mission, headed by 'some person of economic and foreign experience', such as Mr. Henry Grady, who had recently visited India.[3] At the end of February Bajpai told Berle that the Government of India would enthusiastically welcome such a mission.[4] He hoped that the head would be 'a man of the world', for he might well be of assistance in appraising the various elements involved in the constitutional situation. Berle replied that the U.S. 'could not possibly consider interfering in a development which was primarily of concern to India and to Great Britain'.[5] On 6 March the State Department announced the mission and three days later its composition. Johnson was to be its chairman.

Between 9 March, when the membership of the mission was

[1] Johnson Collection, Alderman Library, University of Virginia.
[2] Berle to Sec. of State, 20 Dec. 1941, FRUS, 1942, i. 593–5.
[3] Memo. by Asst. Chief of Division of Near Eastern Affairs, 23 Jan. 1942, ibid. 595–7.
[4] Memo. by Berle, 28 Feb. 1942, ibid. 609.
[5] Ibid.

announced, and 11 March, when Johnson saw C. H. Shaw, Assistant Secretary of State, to discuss his duties, an important departure occurred in U.S. policy. No sooner had the War Cabinet accepted Cripps's offer to go to India (9 March) than Roosevelt cabled personally to Churchill (10 March) to suggest the creation of a Central Temporary Dominion Government in India.[1] When Johnson met Shaw both knew that Johnson would be going out as far more than the head of a mission on munitions. Johnson raised the question of his title and said he 'thought it would be a good plan for there to be a certain amount of over-lapping between himself and Mr. Wilson', the U.S. diplomatic representative in Delhi with the title of Commissioner.[2] He objected to being called Commissioner, for he was the head of the largest law office south of Philadelphia and in Virginia the title meant 'a conspicuously unsuccessful lawyer'. Shaw suggested Special Representative of the President and told John-son that he would assume duties, as Special Representative at Delhi, 'immediately upon his arrival and that this would take precedence over his work as Chairman of the Mission'. Shaw recorded:

He said this was the first precise information he had had on this point. He asked me whether I thought he could do much with the Nationalists in India. I said I thought that in view of the present situation in India he probably could but that it must be done with the utmost care. He seemed to feel that he had not been given any very positive information about anything.

Later that day, after Shaw had conferred with the Under-Secretary of State, Johnson was told that his title would be Personal Representative of the President.[3] In the evening Wilson was told that the President was appointing Johnson to supersede him.

On 24 March it was announced that, in view of his appoint-ment as Personal Representative of the President, Johnson would be devoting his full time to 'duties near the Government of India at New Delhi'.[4] Grady was appointed head of the technical mission. Johnson's first cable home from Delhi, on

---

[1] Roosevelt to Churchill, 10 Mar. 1942, ibid. 615–16.
[2] Memo. by Shaw, 11 Mar. 1942, ibid. 616–17.
[3] Ibid.
[4] Ibid. 617, n. 32.

Saturday 4 April, was addressed to the President, appealing
for his personal intervention with Churchill to save the Cripps
mission from failure. Roosevelt declined to intercede at this
juncture, but clearly wished to be kept informed of developments.[1] Johnson cabled twice more to him during the following
week.

Cripps first saw Johnson when he called upon him at Viceroy's House before lunch on Easter Saturday. He told Coupland
that 'it was clear ... that he had been sent post-haste ... in
order to lend a hand in achieving an Indian settlement'.
Coupland noted that 'Cripps was humorous on this, and doesn't
doubt his capacity to handle him'. That afternoon Johnson
returned the visit. He reported that Linlithgow had told him
there was no chance of a settlement, which offended Cripps
'since the negotiations were in [his] hands'.[2]

On Sunday Shiva Rao arranged for Nehru to meet Johnson
at Cochin House, the American mission's headquarters. Claiming the President's keen interest in the Indian situation, Johnson
stressed that India would forfeit American sympathy if lives
were lost because of Congress's failure to co-operate in the war.
On Monday morning he gave Cripps an encouraging account
of the talk. In the afternoon, after a meeting with Azad and
Nehru, he told Cripps that on defence he had persuaded them
to accept at least (b) and he hoped, eventually, to get them to
accept (c). Cripps had no doubt briefed him well, on tactics as
well as on the defence problem, and he urged upon the Congress
leaders the folly of forfeiting the support of their best friend in
England. Cripps heartily welcomed Johnson's intervention in
the negotiations and told Coupland that 'if a settlement is
achieved it will be largely Johnson's doing'.[3]

At 10 a.m. on Tuesday the 7th Azad and Nehru came to see
Cripps, who now gave them his letter on the defence concessions. 'It is zero hour', noted Coupland.[4] When the Congress
leaders left at 11.30 Cripps estimated the betting as 65 to 35 in
favour of acceptance.

Cripps could by no means count on Nehru's support. Nehru

[1] Acting Sec. of State to Johnson, 5 Apr. 1942, ibid. 627–8.
[2] C.D., 4 Apr. 1942. Johnson stayed at Viceroy's House over the Easter week-
end.
[3] C.D., 6 Apr. 1942.
[4] C.D., 7 Apr. 1942.

was, Azad later recalled, weighed down by the 'terrible mental strain'.[1] As he told Johnson, if he and Cripps were negotiators plenipotentiary then they could settle matters easily.[2] But they were agents of principals with a long history of contention and mistrust. Over Easter the bombing of eastern India had begun and Nehru's sympathies were all with a vigorous resistance to Japan. Yet his position in Congress was not so strong that he could appear to be selling out nationalism to serve imperialist purposes. As, in his own words, 'zero hour approaches',[3] his utterances seem modulated according to his audience. On Easter Monday he talked about defence separately to Indian and European journalists. To the former he said: 'It is a question of who is to be boss in Defence—Englishmen or Indians.'[4] To the latter he remarked: 'We do not want to interfere at all with the Commander-in-Chief, but only to be able to arouse a mass war effort'. The statements are not irreconcilable, but the tone reflects a conflict of loyalties.

At the Tuesday morning meeting with Cripps Nehru spoke of his 'main difficulty' as 'fear lest, if he accepts office, Gandhi will turn the mass of Congressmen against him'.[5] Coupland was incredulous that Nehru could sincerely imagine Gandhi going to the length of a fast against his old friend: 'The difficulty of carrying Congress is quite new. Is it sincere? . . . Could not Nehru and Rajagopalachari, backed by world-opinion, carry all the young Congressmen on a straight issue? Or is Nehru sincere, but betraying the almost universal Hindu lack of moral courage?' Coupland's judgement fails to understand the delicacy of Nehru's position, which, in its way, was no less precarious than that of Cripps himself. It seems certain that Cripps chose, on this occasion, not to rock the boat further by impressing upon Nehru the precise nature of constitutional relations between the Viceroy and his council.

Nehru went direct from Cripps's house to Cochin House. He had promised Johnson half a day's grace before finally rejecting the Declaration. He indicated that he could not carry Congress on alternative (c) and that the Declaration would be

[1] Azad, *India Wins Freedom*, 77.
[2] C.D., 6 Apr. 1942.
[3] Nehru to Johnson, 7 Apr. 1942, Johnson Collection.
[4] Coupland quoting Spry, C.D., 7 Apr. 1942.
[5] C.D., 7 Apr. 1942.

rejected that afternoon. He asked Johnson to appeal to the President, in Coupland's words, 'to squeeze us'.[1] Of course Johnson had already on Easter Saturday asked Roosevelt to consider further effort with Churchill[2] and he did not now press the request again. Instead, he called upon Cripps to tell him that alternative (c) was unacceptable and to suggest 'dressing the doll up another way', so that (c) might look like (b).[3] Rather than creating a new Indian Defence Member and transferring to him Defence Department matters considered safe by the Commander-in-Chief and the functions of defence co-ordination, the Defence Member should retain all Defence Department functions not transferred to Wavell's War Department. It would then appear that Congress had secured the existing Defence Department for an Indian.

After the interview with Johnson Cripps wrote to Nehru. 'The time has come to fire in a personal appeal,' he remarked to Coupland:[4]

[7 April 1942]

My Dear Jawaharlal,

Let me make a final appeal to you, upon whom rests the great burden of decision—a decision so far-reaching in its bearing upon the future relations of our two peoples that its magnitude is indeed portentous.

We can and must carry our people through to friendship and cooperation—I in my sphere, you in yours.

The chance which now offers cannot recur. Other ways may come if this fails but never so good a chance to cement the friendship of our people.

Leadership—the sort of leadership you have—can alone accomplish the result. It is the moment for the supreme courage of a great leader to face all the risks and difficulties—and I know they are there—to drive through to the desired end.

I know your qualities, and your capacity and I beg you to make use of them now.

Yours always affectionately,
Stafford.[5]

[1] Ibid.
[2] Johnson to Roosevelt, 4 Apr. 1942, FRUS, 1942, i. 626–7.
[3] C.D., 7 Apr. 1942.
[4] Ibid.
[5] Nehru, Old Letters, 468.

After lunch, with Cripps's blessing, Johnson saw Wavell alone about 'dressing the doll up another way'.

Wavell at first arbitrarily refused to consider any change in Cripps' amended proposal, in my opinion because he is tired, discouraged and depressed and hates and distrusts Nehru. With the greatest simplicity, and I hope with tact, I explained setup of our own defense establishment of today and convinced him that His Majesty's Government had nothing to lose by reversing form of approach. After he got off his high horse Wavell's approval and cooperation were complete.[1]

Wavell phoned Linlithgow for an appointment and took Johnson with him. Linlithgow was not opposed to considering the allocation of the Defence Department to an Indian, provided the Commander-in-Chief's powers were secured. But the snag in the specification of the functions to be transferred was that anything not specified was left, perhaps inadvertently, with an Indian. It was agreed that the formula needed close scrutiny, and Linlithgow entrusted the task to Hodson, in consultation with the secretaries of the Defence and Legislative Departments. Cripps and his staff would return that night for further discussions. If agreement were reached, Johnson would propose the formula to Congress as likely to command Roosevelt's approval.[2]

Cripps was 'very gay at tea-time' when he returned home and told Coupland of the development. 'Thus', noted Coupland, 'the barometer goes up again.'[3] Personally, he still had misgivings about the effect that the War Cabinet's rigid insistence on the constitution of the executive would have upon Congress. He had written the day before:

I anticipate some difficulty as to the definition of the manner in which the new Government will operate. Will not Congress insist on some assurances *re* 'Cabinet Government', and can the Viceroy give them in a sufficiently convincing form? Surely he can only say, 'I will do my best to treat the Council as a Cabinet'. He has obligations to H.M.G. *re* (1) Foreign Affairs, (2) the Princes, (3) the minorities, and (4) the Services.

Cripps had never told him of the Viceroy's antagonism on the

[1] Johnson to Sec. of State, 9 Apr. 1942, FRUS, 1942, i. 630.
[2] Pinnell's Diary, 7 Apr. 1942, C.M., 547.   [3] C.D., 7 Apr. 1942.

matter, and Coupland erroneously assumed that they agreed on it.[1] After the morning meeting he was unable to elicit from Cripps 'what Nehru thinks re "Cabinet".'[2] At tea-time, when he asked 'if Nehru had raised the "Cabinet" question, Cripps said that they were realists and knew that, if once there was a National Government composed of party-leaders, it would be very difficult for the Viceroy to override them. If they resigned he would be helpless.'

Late Tuesday night—between midnight and 2 a.m.— Linlithgow and Cripps agreed a draft of the new defence formula. It overcame the snag of specifying the functions to be transferred from the Defence to the War Department by listing instead those to be retained by the Defence Department. It was slipped under Johnson's door. It was intended that Johnson would hand it to Nehru, and, if Congress approved it, the formula would be presented as a suggestion by Congress for British approval. Though Linlithgow thought Johnson 'a very pleasant fellow and evidently of good calibre', he would be 'relieved if we get through this business without some misunderstanding or confusion arising on account of [his] activities and perhaps on the part of the President himself'.[3] His apprehensions were soon justified.

At 7.30 on Wednesday morning (8 April) Johnson gave Nehru the formula and at 10.15 he saw Azad. The C.W.C. was in session during the morning, in the latter part of which it 'sent an urgent message to Gandhi'.[4] During the afternoon Nehru wrote and took to Johnson a letter outlining a fresh proposal, which, at about 6 p.m., Johnson showed to Cripps. Nehru proposed that instead of listing the functions to be retained by the Defence Department the formula should list those to be transferred to the Commander-in-Chief's War Department. Cripps accepted the proposal and redrafted the formula, appending a list of the transferred functions. Hodson, who was present, took copies to Linlithgow and Wavell at 7.15. However, Cripps allowed Johnson to take a copy of this Cripps–Johnson formula to Nehru, prior to its consideration by the Viceroy or the Commander-in-Chief.

---

[1] C.D., 6 Apr. 1942.   [2] C.D., 7 Apr. 1942.
[3] Linlithgow to Amery, 7 Apr. 1942, C.M., 550.
[4] Pinnell's Diary, 8 Apr. 1942, MS., loc. cit. 57.

When Cripps saw him at 10 p.m. Linlithgow was not yet aware that Congress had seen the formula.[1] Neither Linlithgow nor his departmental secretaries had examined it fully, but Linlithgow took objection to its provision that disputes over the allocation of functions between the Defence and War Departments should be referred to His Majesty's Government. This was a serious invasion of the Governor-General's powers, he believed. Cripps argued that as the bargain was between the British Government and the Indian parties Britain should arbitrate in order to avoid imputations of viceregal prejudice. Linlithgow was nervous, too, over the specification of the transferred functions without a corresponding list of the retained ones. Cripps countered that the transferred list was one that Linlithgow's own staff had produced when the formula was under discussion the previous night. Linlithgow could rightly claim that Cripps was not, on that account, justified in assuming that he would accept it in the context of the new Cripps–Johnson formula. When, in the course of conversation, Linlithgow realized that Cripps had short-circuited him he was exceedingly, and reasonably, angry. He berated Cripps severely. By allowing the C.W.C. to see the formula Cripps had virtually foreclosed the matter: how could the Viceroy resist a formula agreed by Cripps, the U.S.A., and Congress?

Late in the night of Wednesday 8 April Cripps was hopeful of success. Johnson had told him that the C.W.C.s' voting on the original defence alternative (c) had been 7 to 5 against; on the morning's formula it was even; on the final Cripps–Johnson formula it had become 7 to 5 in favour. Nehru's letter to Johnson had said that given a real national government India would fight to the full. Johnson's latest estimate of the odds was 20 to 1 in favour. Even as he emerged from Linlithgow's wigging Cripps remained buoyant. At 1 a.m. on 9 April he cabled to Churchill: 'Largely owing to very efficient and wholehearted help of Col. Johnson, President Roosevelt's personal respresentative, I have hopes scheme may now succeed. I should like you to thank the President for Col. Johnson's help on behalf of H.M.G. and also personally on my own behalf.'[2]

After Cripps left him Linlithgow cabled to Amery in high

---

[1] Linlithgow's Note, 8 Apr. 1942, C.M., 553.
[2] C.M., 556.

dudgeon.[1] He mentioned his 'own strong feeling of grievance',
the 'issue of . . . consistency with instructions of War Cabinet',
and the danger of Congress manœuvres driving a wedge
between Britain and the U.S.A. He would nevertheless do his
best with the formula if Wavell accepted it, 'for we cannot run
the risk of the Governor-General, the Chief and His Majesty's
Government being shown as unwilling to honour a formula
agreed between His Majesty's Government's emissary and
Roosevelt's personal representative, if that formula secures the
support not only of Congress but of the Muslim League'. In the
early hours of morning the grievance still rankled with him and
he cabled again to Amery.[2] He began, 'You can imagine my own
feelings', but proceeded to disclaim any wish to obstruct the
working of the formula, if Wavell and the War Cabinet accepted
it.

Cripps saw Linlithgow at 12.15 on Thursday. Azad and
Nehru were to come to him at 5.30. Johnson had said that the
C.W.C. were 'going to accept on last night's formula'.[3] He had
received a letter from Nehru not inconsistent with that inference.[4]
Cripps learned from Linlithgow that Wavell was prepared to
accept the formula subject to some modifications, which Cripps
felt he could present to Congress as merely changes of expression. Linlithgow intimated his provisional acquiescence but insisted that as he had not seen the formula before it had gone
to Congress he could accept no responsibility for it.

The operation of the Cripps–Johnson axis behind Linlithgow's
back embittered the Viceroy. As if to emphasize that Cripps
could not look to him for support in his final negotiations for a
settlement, Linlithgow sent a note to Cripps early in the afternoon:

Before your interview with Congress leaders this afternoon I think I
should draw your attention to . . . the Secretary of State's [stipula-
tions of 6 April] . . . that the constitutional position of the Viceroy's
Council cannot be altered, and the emphasis laid by the War Cabinet
on the necessity of avoiding misunderstanding between yourself and
Indian political leaders on this point. In view of the desirability of

[1] Linlithgow to Amery, 9 Apr. 1942, C.M., 557.
[2] C.M., 561.
[3] Pinnell's Diary, 9 Apr. 1942, C.M., 562.
[4] Nehru to Johnson, 9 Apr. 1942, Johnson Collection.

avoiding any possible recrimination between the Governor-General and the future Executive Council on the matter I trust you will be able to make the position clear.[1]

At lunch-time pressmen learned from Rajaji as he was leaving the C.W.C. that the Cripps–Johnson formula had been accepted, subject to some verbal amendments. At tea-time Cripps and Coupland discussed whether the Chief Justice or the Governor of Bombay should stand in as acting Viceroy 'if there is to be a change'.[2]

[1] C.M., 570.
[2] C.D., 9 Apr. 1942.

5

THE SECOND OFFER REJECTED, REVIVED, AND REJECTED
(April 1942–June 1945)

(i) *The Failure of the Mission*

ON THURSDAY 9 April Nehru and Azad came to see Cripps at
5.30 p.m. and stayed until 8. The first hour was spent discussing
the Cripps–Johnson formula, especially the first paragraph:

(a) The Defence Department shall be placed in the charge of a
representative Indian Member, but certain functions relating
to the conduct of the war will be exercised, until the new constitution comes into operation, by the Commander-in-Chief,
who will be in control of the war activities of the armed forces
in India, and who will be a member of the Executive Council
for that purpose.[1]

At the Congressmen's request Cripps omitted the words 'until
the new constitution comes into operation', thereby implying
that the functions transferred to the Commander-in-Chief
would revert to the Defence Department after the war. However, to meet Wavell's criticisms, Cripps also omitted the words
'for that purpose', which had seemed to suggest that Wavell
might only attend the executive meetings on occasions appropriate to his wartime functions. Nehru and Azad argued that
'the C.-in-C. was only to attend if he were sent for' and wanted
to know 'would the C.-in-C. do this, that, and the other?'[2]
  The question merged into the more general matter of the
operation of the council. In view of the Linlithgow–Churchill

---

[1] In Linlithgow to Amery, 9 Apr. 1942, C.M., 559.
[2] C.D., 9 Apr. 1942; Coupland's note on a talk with Cripps on 5 June 1942,
Appx. II to C.D.

axis against a quasi-Cabinet Cripps could give no undertaking on this point. When Nehru called for 'verbal undertakings or conventions as to what would happen' Cripps could say only that 'it was a matter for them to discuss with the Viceroy. They should take the power and make the most of it, aware as they were how difficult it would be for the Viceroy to override them.'[1] He insisted that

the operation of the Government was for the Viceroy to decide and that there could be no major change in the constitution. All the earlier suggestions as to the quasi-Cabinet procedure he had himself made had been subject to the condition 'within the existing constitution'.[2]

Coupland observed that 'C. was somewhat depressed at the end of the long sitting'.[3] Nehru had 'made clear his reluctance to work with the Viceroy and the old G[overnment] of I[ndia] machine'. The C.W.C. would meet again the next day and give a final reply by the evening.

At their interview on Thursday night Linlithgow asked whether, pursuant to his letter of that afternoon, Cripps had protected the Viceroy's statutory position. Cripps assured him that he had refused to argue or define the point, had talked of 'national government and had avoided any mention of cabinet government'.[4] But he had said that 'the Viceroy would doubtless do all he could by means of appropriate conventions'. Linlithgow 'did not like the general position'. He 'could not see how it was possible to reconcile a convention of that kind with the written constitution and with the precise instructions of H.M.G. to preserve the position. He would have a bad time in preserving the position.' As Linlithgow realized, Cripps was imposing upon him the onus for 'wrecking . . . the wonderful settlement arrived at by Sir Stafford Cripps', if Congress accepted the Declaration subject to viceregal assurances on the working of the council as a Cabinet.

Overnight, Cripps might still hope that with the co-operation of Congress and the help of American pressure the resistance of Linlithgow and Churchill to the idea of a quasi-Cabinet might

[1] C.D., 9 Apr. 1942.   [2] C.D., Appx. II.
[3] C.D., 9 Apr. 1942.   [4] Pinnell's Note, 9 Apr. 1942, C.M., 571.

be broken. On the morning of Friday the 10th, however, the Linlithgow–Churchill alliance appeared to have triumphed and the Cripps–Johnson formula to be doomed. Churchill was determined to cut Cripps down and Cripps's indiscretion had given him the necessary weapon.

When Churchill received the Cripps–Johnson formula early on Thursday morning he arranged for the India Committee to scrutinize it at 11 a.m. and report to the War Cabinet at noon. Pending the decision he prohibited Cripps from committing London to the formula, on which the War Cabinet must have the independent opinions of Linlithgow and Wavell.[1] As the Cripps–Johnson formula was an advance on Cripps's alternative (c), so the issue must again be reviewed. This instruction awaited Cripps when he awoke on Friday morning.

At 10.30 a.m. Thursday Churchill received Harry Hopkins, Special Adviser and assistant to President Roosevelt, in the Cabinet Room. He read out Linlithgow's account of the Cripps–Johnson formula and its negotiation behind his back. Hopkins realized that if the noon Cabinet meeting rejected a formula ostensibly approved by the President then Roosevelt might be sorely embarrassed. He therefore made a diplomatic but erroneous disclaimer:

I told the Prime Minister that Johnson's original mission to India had nothing whatever to do with the British proposals and that I was very sure that he was not acting as the representative of the President in mediating the Indian business. That I believed Cripps was using Johnson for his own ends, Cripps being very anxious to bring Roosevelt's name into the picture. That it was to Cripps' interest to get Roosevelt identified with his proposals. I told Mr. Churchill of the President's instructions to me, namely that he would not be drawn into the Indian business except at the personal request of the Prime Minister and then only if he had an assurance both from India and Britain that any plan that he worked out would be acceptable. . . . Churchill at once wrote in longhand a cable to the Viceroy stating that he was sure Johnson was not acting as personal representative of the President in negotiations between the Indian Congress and Cripps.[2]

[1] Churchill to Cripps, 9 Apr. 1942, C.M., 563.
[2] Hopkins's notes on meeting with Churchill, 10.30–12, 9 Apr. 1942, in Cabinet Room, quoted in R. E. Sherwood, *Roosevelt and Hopkins, An Intimate History* (New York, 1948), 524.

Though it is true that Roosevelt had cabled to Johnson on 4 April that he did not wish to intercede personally at that juncture, the facts of Johnson's appointment contradict Hopkins's disclaimer. Certainly, too, he suffered no rebuke for freely using the President's name during his mediation, even though he concluded his account of it with the words: 'The magic name over here is Roosevelt.'[1] Hopkins explained his disclaimer in a cable to the President: 'I have told the Prime Minister and Eden that [whatever] Johnson . . . is doing he is doing at the specific request of Cripps. . . . I believe it important that Johnson's part in this be played down because of the danger of a proposal being made to the British Government which they might reject and which the public might think comes from you.'[2]

Churchill put his own gloss upon Hopkins's words. As the War Cabinet began to arrive he sent off a cable to Cripps, which also awaited him on Friday morning.

Colonel Johnson is not President Roosevelt's personal representative in any matter outside the specific mission dealing with Indian munitions. . . . I feel sure President would be vexed if he, the President, were to seem to be drawn into the Indian constitutional issue. His message [sic] to me, just received from Mr. Hopkins, who is with me as I write, was entirely opposed to anything like U.S. intervention or mediation.[3]

Yet within forty-eight hours Roosevelt was cabling Hopkins to urge Churchill immediately to rescue the Cripps mission—by then beyond salvation.

The India Committee members of the War Cabinet filed into the Cabinet Room from their meeting next door at 11 Downing Street, where no conclusions had been reached. Churchill read out to the War Cabinet the two cables that he had sent to Cripps that morning. It seemed as though Cripps was drawing in the head of an American munitions mission as mediator between the British Government and Congress, was falsely claiming that he represented the President, and was bypassing the Viceroy and the Commander-in-Chief on the vital matter of defence. The Cripps–Johnson formula was

[1] Johnson to Sec. of State, 9 Apr. 1942, FRUS, 1942, i. 630.
[2] Hopkins to Roosevelt, ibid. 629–30.
[3] Churchill to Cripps, 9 Apr. 1942, C.M., 564.

objectionable in its disregard for the Viceroy's right to settle disputes over the allocation of defence functions and its derogation
from the Commander-in-Chief's position as a full member of
the executive.

The War Cabinet meeting was harshly critical of Cripps. On
the facts presented it was impossible for Attlee to dissent from
the need for a firm line, though he must have been dismayed by
the extent of the reaction. Some of his colleagues objected to
Cripps's promised Indianization of the executive, believing
that without his official members on the executive, and without
a spokesman in the legislature, the Viceroy would be in an
impossible position.[1]

Besides Churchill's cables, Cripps received two from the
War Cabinet on Friday morning. One expressed objections to
the Cripps–Johnson formula. The other rebuked him for
negotiating it behind Linlithgow's back, called for a clear
account of developments under paragraph (e) which Cripps,
the Viceroy, and the Commander-in-Chief were propounding,
inquired about the meaning of 'National Government as
though the members of it would all be Indians', and put an end
to Cripps's capacity to negotiate: 'It is essential to bring the
whole matter back to Cabinet's plan which you went out to
urge, with only such amplifications as are agreed to be put
forward.'[2]

Coupland records that he found 'gloom at H.Q.' when he
arrived after breakfast on Friday morning.[3] Cripps now knew
that Linlithgow had been cabling home behind his back to
complain of his proceedings: 'Cripps has shown the V. every
cable he has sent on the negotiations, and resents the V. not
having done the same.' Cripps took a high line in reply to
Churchill's and the War Cabinet's strictures: 'Your telegrams
. . . apparently refer to some sent from here which I have not
seen, and therefore I find difficulty in understanding them.'[4]
He related the history of the Cripps–Johnson formula and
answered criticisms of it. He claimed that there had never been
any departure from the Declaration and that the term 'National

---

[1] War Cabinet, 9 Apr. 1942, C.M., 566.
[2] War Cabinet to Cripps, 9 Apr. 1942, C.M., 567.
[3] C.D., 10 Apr. 1942.
[4] Cripps to War Cabinet, 10 Apr. 1942, C.M., 577.

Government' was suggested to him by Linlithgow. He concluded:

I am sorry that my colleagues appear to distrust me over this matter and I am quite prepared to hand the matter over if they would rather someone else carried on the negotiations.

I have throughout told you that I would not agree anything that was not satisfactory to Commander-in-Chief and Viceroy on the Defence question, but this you seem to doubt. Unless I am trusted I cannot carry on with the task.

A further reason for Cripps's gloom was that Johnson had brought a discouraging letter that Nehru had written him the previous night:

We have just come back, the Congress President and I, after two and a half hours' talk with Sir Stafford Cripps. I am very sorry to say that the talk was entirely unsatisfactory. Of course we shall consider everything that Sir Stafford Cripps said carefully tomorrow and not come to a hasty decision.

It was not just the wording of the formula in regard to Defence. One could come to an agreement about this. But the whole picture that emerged from our talks took me aback and I suddenly discovered that the very premises on which we had been discussing this subject during the last four days were unjustified. The whole structure that we had tried to build up so laboriously in our minds was without any real foundation.[1]

Cripps could only tell Johnson that there was then nothing more he could do, for his powers had been rescinded: 'Cripps with embarrassment told me that he could not change original draft declaration without Churchill's approval and that Churchill has cabled him that he will give no approval unless Wavell and Viceroy separately send their own code cables unqualifiedly endorsing any change Cripps wants.'[2] That day the fate of the mission depended upon the Viceroy and Congress. Spry was making arrangements for the Crippery's departure at 8 a.m. on the Sunday.

Cripps spent a long drawn-out afternoon waiting for the Congress reply.[3] Soon after 2 p.m. two members of the executive,

[1] Nehru to Johnson, 9 Apr. 1942, Johnson Collection.
[2] Johnson to Roosevelt, 11 Apr. 1942, FRUS, 1942, i. 631–2.
[3] C.D., 10 Apr. 1942.

Aney and N. R. Sarkar, saw Pinnell separately. Both told of a likely breakdown in negotiations and Aney suggested that Linlithgow talk with Cripps and Nehru. Linlithgow declined to act.

Azad's letter of rejection arrived at Cripps's house at 7 p.m. Cripps read it as his staff looked on in silence. He was outwardly unmoved and said little except to read out the crucial sentences:

Unfortunately to our disadvantage you had referred both privately and in the course of public statements to a National Government and a Cabinet consisting of Ministers. These words have a certain significance and we had imagined that the new government would function with full powers as a Cabinet with the Viceroy acting as a constitutional head; but the new picture that you placed before us [yesterday] was really not very different from the old, the difference being one of degree and not of kind. The new government could neither be called, except vaguely and inaccurately, nor could it function as a National Government. It would just be the Viceroy and his Executive Council with the Viceroy having all his old powers. We did not ask for any legal changes but we did ask for definite assurances and conventions which would indicate that the new government would function as a free government, the members of which act as members of a Cabinet in a constitutional government. . . . We were informed that nothing could be said at this stage even vaguely and generally about the conventions that should govern the new government and the Viceroy. This was a matter in the Viceroy's sole discretion and at a later stage it could be discussed directly with the Viceroy. . . . The peril that faces India affects us more than it can possibly affect any foreigner and we are anxious and eager to do our utmost to face it and overcome it. But we cannot undertake responsibilities when we are not given the freedom and power to shoulder them. . . .[1]

The terms of the rejection could not have surprised Agatha Harrison and Horace Alexander, whose insight into the minds of the national leaders they so evidently reveal.

The reply still expressed willingness to 'assume responsibility provided a truly National Government is formed', but it must be a 'Cabinet Government with full power and must not merely be a continuation of the Viceroy's Executive Council'. However, since that morning Cripps had been powerless to move,

[1] Azad to Cripps, 10 Apr. 1942, C.M., 587.

while Linlithgow and Churchill worked together to hammer the nails into the mission's coffin.

Early on the 10th Linlithgow cabled to Amery that in their interview following his final meeting with Nehru and Azad Cripps had failed to give him 'assurance that the position of the Governor-General had not been compromised during negotiations in regard to his powers and duties'.[1] Linlithgow was adamantly opposed to working his executive as a Cabinet: 'This is a matter on which I must know with precision what are the instructions of His Majesty's Government to which I am to work. It is really no use trying to shuffle round this difficulty. Either the Governor-General must continue to have the right to differ from his colleagues ... or he must promise that in no circumstances will he refuse to act upon their advice.' The hyperbolic 'in no circumstances' mirrors the mind of a man unaccustomed to the processes of conciliation, co-operation, and corporate management. Cripps had never suggested the abrogation of the Viceroy's powers and duties. However, his colleagues in London received the cable in circumstances that caused them to give credence to Linlithgow's imputation. In negotiating the Cripps–Johnson formula and in his readiness to have disputes over defence functions referred back to London he did seem to be undermining Linlithgow's position.

At 3.30 p.m. on Friday 10 April the India Committee met to consider the Cripps–Johnson formula, together with Cripps's response to the rebuke. A cable approving the formula, subject to the agreement of Wavell and Linlithgow, and the modification of the disputes clause, was drafted. At this stage Linlithgow's cable on his powers and duties arrived. Churchill summoned the Committee to 10 Downing Street, where he took the chair and commanded the proceedings. The Committee agreed to the explicit repudiation of Cripps's powers of negotiation, the reassurance of the Viceroy as to his position, and the delivery of an objectionable *coup de grâce* by Churchill himself.

A cable in the name of the War Cabinet was sent to Linlithgow with a copy to Cripps: 'There can be no question of any convention limiting in any way your powers under the existing constitution. ... If Congress leaders have gathered impression

[1] C.M., 578.

that such a new convention is now possible this impression should be definitely removed.'[1] In relation to defence functions the Viceroy must retain his powers of allotting them as between portfolios: 'The Viceroy cannot be considered, apart either from the Government of India or His Majesty's Government, merely as a party in a dispute with Congress.' Churchill himself dealt directly with Cripps:

We feel that in your natural desire to reach a settlement with Congress you may be drawn into positions far different from any the Cabinet and Ministers of Cabinet rank approved before you set forth. . . . We have been told nothing about the character and composition of the new Council or National Government you think should be formed. . . . We are concerned about the Viceroy's position. . . . You speak of carrying on negotiations. It was certainly agreed between us all that there were not to be negotiations but that you were to try to gain acceptance with possibly minor variations or elaborations of our great offer which has made so powerful an impression here and throughout the United States.[2]

The cable was a distorted account of the basis of the mission. It betrays Churchill's own misunderstanding of the powers that Cripps took with him and his own satisfaction that the mission had served the real purpose for which he accepted it—the neutralization of pro-Congress sympathies in the U.S.A. and in his own government.

Coupland found Cripps 'very calm and friendly' after he had read these cables early on Saturday morning.[3] 'Not generous,' recorded Coupland of Churchill's cable, 'suggesting that Cripps [was] "negotiating" outside his brief, whereas in fact he has never gone beyond elucidation of the Declaration.'

(ii) Post-mortem

The Cripps mission was crushed by the monolithic millstones of Churchillian Conservatism and Congress nationalism.

Cripps set out to establish an Indianized national or quasi-Cabinet government, whose advice the Viceroy would normally accept, but whom he must, because of his special responsi-

---

1 War Cabinet to Linlithgow, 10 Apr. 1942, C.M., 581.
2 Churchill to Cripps, 10 Apr. 1942, C.M., 582.
3 C.D., 11 Apr. 1942.

bilities, ultimately have power to override. He was consistent in this objective from first to last. At the outset he knew that Linlithgow would dislike such a reform and that his own Conservative colleagues would uphold his opposition. He had tried and failed to dislodge Linlithgow in February. He could not offer Congress a quasi-Cabinet with an assurance of viceregal and War Cabinet support. But if he could win from Congress agreement to enter the government provided assurance were given that it would observe cabinet conventions, then he might, on the strength of it, expect to extract the consent of the War Cabinet and either the acquiescence or resignation of Linlithgow.

Coupland, the constitutional historian and independent observer of the mission, saw the tragic irony in Churchill's onslaught against Cripps's readiness to throw away the Viceroy's legal powers whereas Nehru was complaining of his obdurate defence of them. In the immediate aftermath of failure, on the journey home, Coupland noted:

For five years in some Provinces and for two in Congress Provinces [the Governors] have operated quasi-Cabinet Government with considerable success: i.e. they have very rarely overridden their Ministers and have nearly always succeeded in discharging their 'special responsibilities' by tact and persuasion. But the power to override has always been there. . . . The fact is that, besides military control, an irreducible amount of civil control must . . . remain in British hands until the final and complete transfer of power is effected. With mutual trust and goodwill a quasi-Cabinet system could be worked at the Centre as it has been worked in the Provinces.[1]

In 1937 Linlithgow had paved the way for Congress to enter provincial government by giving an assurance upon the Governor's exercise of his special responsibilities under the India Act:

Before taking a decision against the advice of his Ministers . . . a Governor will spare no pains to make clear to his Ministers the reasons which have weighed with him in thinking both that the decision is one which it is incumbent on him to take, and that it

[1] 'The Impracticability of Full Cabinet Government at Present', 12 Apr. 1942, in C.D., 282–5.

is the right one. . . . In such circumstances, given the goodwill which we can I trust postulate on both sides . . . conflicts need not in a normal situation be anticipated.[1]

The Viceroy had a further statutory obligation, to override his council on any matter 'whereby the safety, tranquillity or interest of British India' may be affected. He could not, of course, undertake not to exercise such powers. But he could, as he did for the provinces in 1937, have offered assurances upon the spirit in which special responsibilities and powers would be regarded.

There is a good deal of testimony to suggest that Congress was prepared to enter a government on the basis of an assurance on quasi-Cabinet government, and that until the fateful final interview with Cripps on 9 April Nehru and Azad assumed that Cripps was the War Cabinet's emissary bearing that assurance.

On 8 April Nehru said to the cartoonist, Shankar, 'In a few days' time you will be drawing war cartoons and backing up a "National Government". I think we are very near agreement.'[2] On Sunday the 12th he told the press that he had gone to Cripps on the Thursday seventy-five per cent confident of agreement.[3] The *Hindustan Times*, which was financed by Birla and edited by Gandhi's son, Devadas, lamented:

The Congress demand for a National Government did not involve any amendment of the present constitution except for the provision regarding those members in the Viceroy's Executive Council with 10 years' service under the Crown. In other respects, the Congress was ready to join the present Executive Council as it was. All that it wanted was a previous understanding with the Viceroy, by convention, that he would accept the advice of this Government ordinarily and would not overrule its decisions, except on rare occasions, in which case the remedy of resignation would be open to the Government. . . . The statutory powers of veto which the Viceroy now possesses would continue to vest in him and he would not hesitate to use them when he felt it necessary to do so.[4]

Congressman Satyamurti believed that all would have been well if Cripps had arranged a personal discussion between

[1] Broadcast by Viceroy, 22 June 1937, Gwyer and Appadorai, *Documents*, i. 395–6.
[2] Hodson to Coupland, 8 May 1942, C.D., Appx. I.
[3] Shiva Rao, *India's Freedom Movement*, 181.
[4] 5 May 1942, quoted in Hodson to Coupland, 8 May 1942, loc. cit.

Azad, Nehru, and Linlithgow. Sapru similarly blamed the Viceroy's aloofness for Cripps's failure:

All these technical difficulties [over the letter of the constitution] could have been got over if the Viceroy had not kept himself behind the *Purdah*. I cannot imagine any great Viceroy with any sense of appreciation of the danger behaving in this manner. His whole life at Delhi reminds me of the idols in Hindu temples which are visible to their worshippers only at certain times. If he had only stepped forward and invited Congress leaders and Muslim leaders and spoken to them only a word of encouragement and advised them to come into Government that alone, in my opinion, would have altered the attitude of these leaders.[1]

It was essentially because of their suspicion of Linlithgow that the Congress demanded assurances from Cripps of the concession of quasi-Cabinet government. Some time later an English visitor questioned Nehru about the mission's failure and reported

that with a more accessible person with whom the Congress leaders could have talked round the table and discussed actually how the Executive worked, they might possibly have accepted. A member of the Executive seems to have told him that things there were very much cut and dried and that the Executive expected to sign on the dotted line. Europeans and Indians generally complained that the Viceroy kept to himself, Laithwaite and a very small inner circle.[2]

Even after the C.W.C. had decided upon rejection Congress left the door open for negotiations to continue. Azad's letter to Cripps still offered co-operation in a truly national government. Nehru carefully kept Johnson informed of his accessibility by phone or messenger, and Johnson continued confident that a quasi-Cabinet would win Congress over.[3] Rajaji quizzed Hodson on Cripps's sudden departure and claimed that he had misjudged the situation. Azad's letter 'was not meant to be final. . . . It left room for discussion on some important matters. Cripps should at least have explained personally . . . what the point of difference over a National Government was, and why a break

[1] Sapru to Sir Jagdish Prasad, 19 Apr. 1942, Sapru Collection on microfilm, reel 19, p. 254, Australian National Library.
[2] Note by Sir D. T. Monteath, Perm. U. Sec. of State for India, on conversation with Sir E. Villiers of Ministry of Information, 13 Aug. 1942, on Villiers's visit to Nehru on 5 July 1942, L/PO/6/105e. See also Villiers's memo. of conversation with Nehru, 5 July 1942, ibid.
[3] Johnson Collection.

was necessary.'[1] Of course, by then Cripps knew, as Linlithgow wrote explicitly, that Linlithgow would 'not have stood for' the introduction of the convention of Cabinet government 'save under direct instructions',[2] and that the War Cabinet would not issue any such instructions.

Cripps knew from the start of the antagonism of Linlithgow and Churchill to a quasi-Cabinet and he accepted it as a hazard of his mission. He resented Linlithgow's secret cables, which did much to sabotage his negotiations, and he was wounded by Churchill's mistrust. Yet his long experience of their illiberality led him to expect the worst from them. Despite the machiavellianism of the Viceroy and the opportunism and tergiversation of the Prime Minister he respected their patriotism and courage and accepted their contrary position as a given element in the situation. He bore with remarkable loyalty the destruction of his mission without, in fact, uttering a word of public recrimination. He never even told Coupland that Linlithgow was opposed to a quasi-Cabinet, so that Coupland was left sincerely believing, as he was to write, that Congress rejected a scheme for a quasi-Cabinet advanced by Cripps and supported by Linlithgow.

Cripps reserved his criticisms for Congress. As he awaited the C.W.C.'s decision on Friday 10 April he told Coupland that 'the difficulty now was only distrust, distrust of co-operating with people whose response was not whole-hearted, fear of being obstructed and defeated by officials etc. "They have come to the very edge of the water, and stripped, but hesitate to make the plunge because the water looks so cold." '[3] Cripps felt that Congress should take the power offered and make the most of it. He felt that he was offering it real power if only it would undertake to accept it. He himself had entered Churchill's War Cabinet as an individual and he had staked his position there on the achievement of a Congress national government. The Congress leaders seemed unprepared to go half as far for their own sake. He regarded them as allies who deserted their joint cause.

[1] Hodson to Coupland, 8 May 1942, loc. cit.
[2] Linlithgow to Amery, 23 Apr. 1942, C.M., 670.
[3] C.D., 10 Apr. 1942. Cf. Villiers's note of Nehru's comment that distrust was the fundamental reason for rejecting Cripps's offer (memo. of 5 July 1942, loc. cit.).

Cripps was conscious that the erosion of his brief by the Linlithgow–Churchill axis left him unable to give Congress members more than his personal expectation that if they entered the government the Viceroy would treat them as members of a Cabinet. Yet he failed to understand that his own enforced backsliding appeared to Nehru and Azad as apostasy, and was a major cause of the Congress rejection. Surprise and dismay characterize the letters of Nehru and Azad when they write of their inability to hold Cripps to his earlier undertakings on quasi-Cabinet government. Yet Cripps, still feeling that a quasi-Cabinet was theirs if they would only trust him, convinced himself that the real cause of the rejection lay elsewhere.

Cripps held that on Wednesday 8 April the Congress leaders were prepared to accept but that they came to meet him on the 9th seeking to provoke a breakdown.[1] Cripps explained the change by the intervention of Gandhi. Early in the negotiations he had convinced himself that if he failed it would be because of Gandhi's opposition to the acceptance of office for war purposes and his influence over the Working Committee. He found sufficient evidence for his hypothesis in Nehru's apprehension of Gandhi's antagonism and in a Government of India intelligence report that on the morning of the 9th there occurred a two-hour telephone conversation between the Congress leaders in Delhi and Gandhi at Wardha.[2]

There is testimony that Gandhi denied intervening after he left Delhi on 4 April with the advice that the C.W.C. should follow Azad. Early in 1943 Horace Alexander wrote to Miss Harrison: '. . . both M. K. G[andhi] and Mahadev [Desai] explicitly told me at the end of June that he had no communication whatever with any member of the Working Committee after he left Delhi. He purposely and deliberately refused to intervene in any way once the working committee had agreed

[1] Coupland's note of conversation with Cripps on 5 June 1942, loc. cit.; Cripps's Report on his Mission, 6 July 1942, *Transfer of Power, II, Quit India* (Q.I.), 227 (pp. 341–2).

[2] I have failed to trace the report in the I.O.L. or the I.N.A. F. F. Turnbull referred to the conversation as a 'known fact' from Government of India 'secret sources'. He thought it 'most unwise to trot . . . out' the fact and was 'not at all convinced' that Azad's letter of 10 April claiming tergiversation did 'not represent the true state of affairs'. Turnbull to Joyce, Patrick, and Monteath, 21 Sept. 1942, L/PO/6/105e.

to consider the proposals.'[1] In September 1942 Rajaji issued a statement denying Gandhi's responsibility for the failure of the mission.[2]

It would not have been uncharacteristic for Gandhi to have stepped aside and left the decision on office acceptance to the C.W.C. After the failure of non-co-operation in 1922 and of civil disobedience in 1934 he was prepared to condone council entry by Swarajists. In 1929 and 1930 he allowed Nehru, as Congress president, to determine policy towards the Irwin declaration and the Sapru–Jayakar peace proposals. He stepped aside over the question of co-operation with the war effort in July 1940 and December 1941, aware that Congress would not accept non-violence as the means of national defence.

It seems unnecessary to appeal to an intervention by Gandhi at the eleventh hour in order to explain the C.W.C.'s rejection. As Coupland realized early in April Cripps looked at the influence of Gandhism in the C.W.C. from a distorting angle. More significant than a non-violent abstention from office was the C.W.C.'s concern that the powers ceded to a national government might be insufficient to enable Congress ministers to discharge the responsibilities they would be held to assume. The influence of Gandhians, or Gandhi himself, may well have contributed to Nehru's close questioning of Cripps about the executive's powers and status on 9 April. It was vital for Nehru to test the water for coldness before committing his colleagues to plunge in, and in their final discussion Nehru found it so icy that to attempt to push the C.W.C. would be more than his position was worth. Indeed, it is clear that Cripps failed to appreciate that Nehru's position was as precarious as that of himself. Nehru, like Cripps, needed an assurance of co-operation from the other side in order to carry his own.

Cripps's misunderstanding and unreasonable expectations of Nehru and Azad explain the asperity of his reply to Azad's letter of rejection.[3] He fixed upon the real substance of the refusal as the claim that 'the form of Government suggested is not such as would enable you to rally the Indian people as you desire'. He charged Congress with demanding, for the first time

[1] Harrison to Cripps, 15 Jan. 1943, I.C.G., Cripps file.
[2] *Bombay Chronicle*, 15 Sept. 1942.
[3] Cripps to Azad, 10 Apr. 1942, C.M., 590.

during the negotiations, a constitutional change to establish a 'Cabinet Government with full power'. Constitutional change had been ruled out from the start, whereas full Cabinet government without it would be an irresponsible and irremovable government, 'an absolute dictatorship of the majority'. Such a government would be rejected by the minorities and was inconsistent with the British government's pledges. The British proposals went 'as far as possible, short of a complete change in the Constitution'.

Azad and Nehru were pained and surprised. Azad responded:

It seems that there has been a progressive deterioration in the British Government's attitude as the negotiations proceeded. What we were told in our very first talk with you is now denied or explained away. You told me then that there would be a National Government which would function as a Cabinet and that the position of the Viceroy would be analogous to that of the King in England vis-à-vis his Cabinet. . . . You have put forward an argument in your letter which at no time during our talks was mentioned by you. You refer to the 'absolute dictatorship of the majority'. It is astonishing that such a statement should be made in this connection and at this stage. This difficulty is inherent in any scheme of a mixed Cabinet formed to meet an emergency, but there are many ways in which it can be provided for. . . . [The question] might have been considered after the main question was decided: that is the extent of power which the British Government would give to the Indian people.[1]

Nehru cabled in chagrin to Krishna Menon:

Cripps made clear early stages he envisaged national cabinet with Viceroy as constitutional head like King subject reservation defence. Discussion therefore centred around defence. . . . Ultimately Cripps stated no substantial change possible also stated no national cabinet with joint responsibility possible nor could assurances be given about use Viceroy's powers intervention veto. This entirely Viceroy's discretion. . . . This entirely different picture from what Cripps originally suggested. Impossible call this national government or evoke enthusiasm people. At no stage during talks any communal or minority difficulty as Congress claiming power responsibility for national government as whole and question formation government deferred. Last letter Cripps surprisingly stated no possible national cabinet with joint responsibility as this means tyrannical majority rule. This . . . most unfair unjustified. . . . His whole approach has

[1] Azad to Cripps, 11 Apr. 1942, C.M., 604.

been wrong and vitiated by communal outlook. Congress went
utmost limit giving up previous objectives in negotiations. Crux of
matter organization national defence on popular mass basis but this
only possible by free national government.[1]

When Louis Johnson finally left Delhi on 15 May he told a
press conference that 'some day there will have to be a Johnson
version of [the Cripps] affair'.[2] On 11 April, knowing of the repudiation of Cripps's powers, he concluded that London wanted
a Congress refusal. He attributed Cripps's failure to Churchill's
intervention when a satisfactory solution seemed certain.[3]

Briefed by Johnson's cable, Roosevelt responded critically to
Churchill's intimation that despite Britain's utmost efforts
Congress had rejected the Cripps offer:

I most earnestly hope that you may find it possible to postpone
Cripps's departure from India until one more final effort has been
made to prevent a breakdown in the negotiations.

I am sorry to say that I cannot agree with the point of view set
forth in your message to me that public opinion in the United
States believes that the negotiations have failed on broad general
issues. The general impression here is quite the contrary. The feeling
is almost universally held that the deadlock has been caused by the
unwillingness of the British Government to concede to the Indians
the right of self-government, notwithstanding the willingness of the
Indians to entrust technical, military and naval defense control to
the competent British authorities. American public opinion cannot
understand why, if the British Government is willing to permit the
component parts of India to secede from the British Empire after the
war, it is not willing to permit them to enjoy what is tantamount to
self-government during the war.[4]

The appeal reached Churchill at 3 a.m. Sunday 12 April, only
ten minutes before Cripps left Delhi. Cripps would be in
Karachi until six o'clock next morning (Indian time), but
Churchill took refuge in the claim that he could not intervene
now without consulting the Cabinet, which was impossible
until Monday. He chose not to show Roosevelt's appeal to his
Cabinet, unless Roosevelt requested him to do so: 'Anything
like a serious difference between you and me would break my

1 Nehru to V. K. K. Menon, 13 Apr. 1942, Home Pol. 225/42.
2 Shiva Rao, *India's Freedom Movement*, 189.
3 Johnson to Roosevelt, 11 Apr. 1942, FRUS, 1942, i. 631–2.
4 Roosevelt to Hopkins, for Churchill, 11 Apr. 1942, ibid. 633–4.

heart and surely deeply injure both our countries at the height of this terrible struggle.'[1] If that were so, one can only speculate upon the fate of the Cripps mission if Roosevelt had sent his appeal a day or two earlier. Bluff and luck, therefore, were important elements in Churchill's reduction of Cripps.

Cripps was only too well aware of the propaganda aspect of the mission, and especially in relation to America. The morning after the Congress rejection he suggested that Coupland write an account of the mission for *Life* magazine. Coupland did not do that, but he did write the pamphlet *The Cripps Mission*, which was severely critical of Congress's rejection of a quasi-Cabinet, a proposal that in the end it had not been offered![2]

Cripps sent Spry to the U.S.A. and Canada, *en route* back to London, 'to assist in propaganda'.[3] In the U.S.A. Spry found widespread suspicion at the most senior official level that the mission had been sabotaged from London. The President asked: 'Some people believe that the mission would have been successful if the instructions had not been changed during the later stages of the negotiations. Can you tell me if there is anything to that—were there any restrictions placed on Cripps' instructions?'[4] The President's Executive Assistant spoke of 'deep-seated suspicion, if not conviction, that at the moment of success, Sir Stafford Cripps received new instructions which made an Indian settlement impossible'.[5] Berle and Mr. Justice Frankfurter of the Supreme Court similarly subscribed to the sabotage theory. Spry kept a very straight bat. He had

seen every telegram, had read all the documents and was in Sir Stafford's confidence. Therefore, [he] could say this interpretation was nonsense. . . . There was no change of instructions, no disagreement between Sir Stafford, the War Cabinet, the Secretary of State, the Viceroy or Commander-in-Chief, and that the final discussions revolved not about principles, but wholly about forms of words, which did not change the principles of the defence proposals.[6]

[1] Churchill to Roosevelt, 12 Apr. 1942, ibid. 634–5.

[2] *Cripps Mission*, 54–62. See also R. G. Coupland, *Indian Politics* (1943), 286 n. 1; I.C.G. Notes, 5 June 1942 (meeting with Coupland).

[3] Cripps's Note on Spry's report on India as a factor in Anglo-American relations, 27 July 1942, Q.I., 339.

[4] Note on interview with Roosevelt, 15 May 1942, L/PO/6/105f.

[5] Note on luncheon with Mr. L. Currie, Exec. Asst. to President, 9 May 1942, ibid.

[6] Note on interview at State Dept. with Dr. S. Hornbeck, 13 May 1942, ibid.

Such disclaimers did nothing to convince senior American opinion. In July the White House still believed that Cripps had been 'torpedoed'.[1]

An American journalist described the fate of the mission. In August Louis Fischer visited India, and his conclusions were close to those reached in the Johnson version. Replying to Spry's disagreement with the articles in the New York *Nation* that embodied his views, he wrote: 'Cripps was stabbed in the back.' The culprits, he added, were 'Englishmen who differed from him'.[2]

(iii) Churchill and the Stopgap Viceroy

The failure of the Cripps mission put at an end any possibility of co-operation between Congress and the British raj in the defence of India. Now Churchill could prevent the constitutional issue being raised for the rest of the war.

A fortnight after Cripps's departure Gandhi was drafting a resolution for the C.W.C. that called for Britain's withdrawal and the adoption of non-violent non-co-operation against any Japanese invasion. Nehru's influence on the Committee enabled him to substitute a draft of his own, less cordial towards Japan. However, unless Roosevelt intervened, as Nehru continued vainly to hope, Congress could now pursue the freedom struggle only as an adversary of Britain. During the following months, as Congress edged toward backing its Quit India demand with a mass non-co-operation movement, Britain followed the now familiar dual course in such circumstances: constitutional policy was reaffirmed and special powers to meet the coming emergency were approved.

At the end of July the War Cabinet agreed, as Linlithgow proposed, that a parliamentary statement of policy was desirable in order to remove Indian apprehension of a retrograde step and to consolidate 'support of moderate and loyal elements behind us against Congress'.[3] Amery drafted a declaration for use in the House of Commons on 30 July:

[1] R. I. Campbell (minister, British Embassy, Washington) to Sir David Scott (Foreign Office), 17 July 1942, ibid. Harry Hopkins was reported to persist in this belief.
[2] See New York *Nation*, 19, 26 Sept. and 14 Nov. 1942.
[3] Linlithgow to Amery, 24 July 1942, Q.I. 316.

His Majesty's Government stand firmly by the broad intention of their offer, which is that on the conclusion of hostilities India shall have it within her power to attain complete self-government through such method of arriving at a constitutional solution and under such form of government as may be agreed among themselves by the principal elements in Indian national life.

The Cabinet rearranged the draft but Amery defeated an attempt by Churchill to qualify 'self-government' by adding 'within the British Commonwealth of Nations', a device 'to whittle down the Cripps Offer'.[1] Amery affirmed in Parliament that the offer stood 'irrespective of the immediate conduct of the Congress'. On the day that Amery rejected Churchill's proposed interpolation, King George VI noted:

[The Prime Minister] amazed me by saying that his colleagues and both, or all three, parties in Parliament were quite prepared to give up India to the Indians after the war. He felt they had already been talked into giving up India. Cripps, the Press and U.S. opinion have all contributed to make their minds up that our rule in India is wrong and has always been wrong for India.[2]

Such statements give a misleading impression of the willingness of Churchill's Cabinet colleagues to accept a full and immediate post-war transfer of power. After the preparation of the Cripps offer Amery had written to Linlithgow:

... in some form or other the Viceroy will have to remain, not merely as constitutional Governor-General, but as representative of broader imperial aspects of government, for a good long time to come, and to be equipped with the instruments of power required to carry out his functions. . . . So whatever else you do or agree to, you had better keep in mind the desirability of retaining Delhi and a considerable area around it as the ultimate federal territory of an eventually united India, and not let it pass into the hands of any one of the 'Dominions' that may temporarily emerge.[3]

Britain would reserve defence for a good while after the transfer of power. Conservatives simply assumed that India would break up after the war and that Britain would remain,

[1] Q.I., 354, 364, 366.
[2] King's Diary, 28 July 1942, J. Wheeler-Bennett, *King George VI: His Life and Reign* (1958), 703.
[3] Letter, 24 Mar. 1942, C.M., 375.

with forces, to provide a central link under the Crown. Linlith-gow regarded self-government and unity as incompatible. In January 1942 he argued against any concession in the central government that 'would make it impossible for us after the war to regain any ground given now, and which we thought it desirable to retrace.'[1] R. A. Butler wrote critically to Amery that the draft declaration did not make clear 'what I am told is implicit in [it], namely that Great Britain has still some role to play in India' after the demission of power upon India's component parts.[2] He thought it impossible for Britain to 'attain in one coup in India what Campbell-Bannerman achieved in South Africa', that is, freedom with unity. At the full Cabinet meeting on 5 March Amery found his colleagues unprepared for the Cripps bombshell, and on 10 April the War Cabinet acquiesced in the repudiation of Cripps's powers to negotiate. In crude terms, the balance of Cabinet opinion favoured the inactive Viceroy rather than the progressive emissary. Cripps failed to get rid of Linlithgow, but Linlithgow was effectively able to get rid of Cripps—with the brisk farewell, 'Goodbye Mr. Cripps!'[3]

Behind the persistent belief in the need for a post-war British presence lay an anti-Congress animus. Churchill regarded Congress as a hostile political element that would paralyse executive action.[4] Amery wrote of Nehru and Gandhi as 'niggling unpractical creatures'.[5] When he expressed doubt 'whether people of that type would ever run straight', Linlith-gow noted: 'They could never run straight. One will have to plough through the old gang down to better and younger stuff.'[6] Linlithgow saw Congress as a party of 'entirely ruthless politicians' who sought only to enhance their own prestige: 'short of acceptance of their full demand no sacrifices however great can be relied on to keep them quiet'.[7] The C.W.C., save Nehru, were a 'collection of declining valetudinarians who have no grip on the country'.[8] Neither Churchill, nor Amery,

[1] Linlithgow to Amery, 21 Jan. 1942, C.M., 23.
[2] Memo. by Butler, 6 Mar. 1942, C.M., 255.
[3] Marginal note on Amery to Linlithgow, 3 Apr. 1942, C.M., 517.
[4] Churchill to Attlee, 7 Jan. 1942, C.M., 6.
[5] Amery to Linlithgow, 2 Feb. 1942, C.M., 58.
[6] Amery to Linlithgow, 3 Apr. 1942; marginal notes by Linlithgow, C.M., 517.
[7] Linlithgow to Amery, 21 Jan. 1942, C.M., 23.
[8] Linlithgow to Amery, 23–27 Jan. 1942, C.M., 30.

nor Linlithgow trusted Congress or wanted it in the executive. None of them wanted to concede any power to Congress.

Roosevelt and the Americans could not reconcile Britain's apparent readiness to grant post-war independence with the refusal to devolve power during the war. Similarly, Coupland puzzled over the quasi-Cabinet question:

> Why should Winston and Amery worry overmuch about this issue? We are going to abdicate in a few years. If Wavell is sure of his own position, what does it matter if the Indian leaders are in virtual control of domestic government? Only a fraction of them will be Congressmen. The Moslems and the minorities will not want to quarrel with us. If Ministers were to push their power too far—to differ with the Viceroy on something really vital, then there would be a show-down, dismissal, and reversion to bureaucratic government. But for that would the heterogeneous Cabinet be able to present a collective front? Surely not.[1]

The truth is that Conservative resistance to a wartime quasi-Cabinet went hand in hand with a persistent unwillingness to accept that the end of the war would bring a complete transfer of power.

The Quit India movement further exacerbated the anti-Congress animus and the prejudice against full post-war independence. On 8 August the A.I.C.C. sanctioned, 'for the vindication of India's inalienable right to freedom and independence, the starting of a mass struggle on non-violent lines on the widest possible scale'.[2] The arguments against such a step had been rehearsed fully in April 1940 and they were even more valid now. Where Muslim minorities governed there were dangers of satyagraha assuming a communal aspect. The British and the Muslims would be driven into a close embrace. Civil disobedience had no hope of wresting India from the British. That such considerations were now set aside indicates the desperation to which exclusion from effective action during three years of war had brought the Congress. The failure of Churchill and Linlithgow to accord it due recognition now made futile rebels and prisoners of the Congress leaders.

On the morning of 9 August, with the approval of the War

[1] C.D., 10 Apr. 1942.
[2] Quit India resolution, Q.I., 470.

Cabinet, Gandhi and the members of the Working Committee were arrested and interned. The provincial and all-India committees of Congress were declared unlawful, their offices and funds were seized, and potential organizers were arrested. Despite this strike to 'render movement abortive by removing its leaders',[1] in August and September the Government of India faced 'the most serious rebellion since that of 1857',[2] with severe disruptions to communications, the need to deploy the equivalent of eight brigades (or fifty-seven battalions) of British troops in aid of the civil authority, and a major dislocation of the war effort. By the end of September Linlithgow reported that 'things are pretty comfortable',[3] though violent disturbances, characteristic of this least Gandhian of the non-co-operation campaigns, persisted for several months.

On the eve of making a parliamentary statement on the situation Churchill held forth in the garden at Downing Street:

I shall tell them that for the last 25 years the Conservative Party has gone on the wrong tracks, it has lost confidence in itself, and it has given way perpetually until the present state of affairs has come about. It is all wrong, thoroughly wrong. If we have ever to quit India, we shall quit it in a blaze of glory, and the chapter that shall be ended then will be the most glorious chapter of that country, not merely in relation to the past but equally in relation to the future, however distant that may be. That will be my statement on India tomorrow. No apology, no quitting, no idea of weakening or scuttling. What do we gain from India? We have lost our trade and all our contracts, we have less than 500 civilians in the whole of the service there . . . and there is only one thing we are doing . . . and that is to do our duty there, and we are prepared to do that at any cost.[4]

His Commons statement on 10 September denied that Congress represented the majority of the people of India, or even the Hindu masses.

On 12 November Cripps suggested to the War Cabinet that Rajaji, the peacemaker on the Indian scene, might be invited to visit London to discuss his plans for Hindu–Muslim unity

[1] Govt. of India Home Dept. to Sec. of State, 3 Aug. 1942, Q.I., 393.
[2] Linlithgow to Churchill, 31 Aug. 1942, Q.I., 662.
[3] Linlithgow to Amery, 21 Sept. 1942, Q.I., 780.
[4] Sir A. R. Mudaliar to Laithwaite, 21 Sept. 1942, *Transfer of Power*, iii. 2.

and a provisional national government. Churchill responded with a 'terrific tirade against the whole conception of Indian self-government'.[1] In a speech at the Mansion House two days earlier he had said crudely: 'We mean to hold our own. I have not become the King's First Minister in order to preside over the liquidation of the British Empire.'[2] In the context of a letter to Linlithgow on Indian policy Amery observed: 'This is, after all, in essence a one-man government, so far as the conduct of the war is concerned, subject to a certain amount of conversation in Cabinet. . . . His greatness . . . is such that we have to accept him as he is.'[3] With Montgomery's victory at El Alamein and the Anglo-American landing in North Africa Churchill was utterly secure as war leader, and he could now dispense with Cripps, who had challenged him unsuccessfully over defence the previous month.

At Churchill's insistence Cripps resigned from the War Cabinet on 22 November and accepted a minor Cabinet office as the Minister of Aircraft Production. Butler commented:

It is clear to all that the politics of Stafford Cripps and Winston Churchill are not alike, and they had some difficulty in running together. The P.M. is tending to turn more and more to the ancient ways and paths of tradition, and Cripps . . . is tending more and more towards a new world of rather undefined and unrestricted socialism. . . . As for our moral position in India—the P.M. has turned towards the traditional, and his speech at Mansion House about not abdicating from the British Empire are trends showing that we should not—to use his own words—'chatter ourselves out of India'.[4]

With Cripps's removal from the War Cabinet it was truer than ever, as Amery was to observe, that while Churchill was Prime Minister there could not be much positive progress with the Indian deadlock.[5]

Churchill long postponed choosing a sucessor to Linlithgow who, by summer 1943, had been Viceroy for almost eight years. For the last three of them Linlithgow's views on India

[1] Amery to Linlithgow, 13 Nov. 1942, ibid. 178.
[2] Speech of 10 Nov. 1942, R. R. James (ed.), *Winston S. Churchill: His Complete Speeches, 1897–1963* (1974), vi. 6688–95.
[3] Amery to Linlithgow, 13 Nov. 1942, loc. cit.
[4] Butler to Hoare, 27 Nov. 1942, Templewood Papers, XIII. 19.
[5] Amery to Hoare, 10 June 1943, ibid.

had accorded so well with Churchill's that he would be difficult to replace. They both espoused a do-nothing policy for the present and looked forward to a post-war British presence. Churchill favoured the eventual solution of the Indian problem whereby 'we might sit on top of a tripos—Pakhistan, Princely India and the Hindus'.[1] This was not very different from Linlithgow's anticipation that Britain would 'carry on with some scheme of government imposed by ourselves with, of course, the inevitable corollary that we shall remain there to hold the balance'.[2] He expected British rule to last another thirty years.

Churchill was determined to appoint a Viceroy who would not precipitate the constitutional issue. Brendan Bracken said that he was 'looking for a tidy administration', and wanted 'not to be bothered'.[3] His choice fell upon Wavell. Butler inferred that this 'must mean that politics are to be put right on one side'.[4] After the war, with two years' experience of working under Churchill (now out of office), Wavell reflected 'I am pretty sure that when he appointed me Viceroy it was with the intention and expectation that I should simply keep things quiet in India till the war was over.'[5] He seemed to have the credentials of a stopgap Viceroy. He had no liking for Congress. He had the greatest admiration for Linlithgow and accepted his imputations that 'Cripps did not play straight over the question of the Viceroy's veto and Cabinet responsibility' and 'was crooked when up against it'.[6] However, very soon after the announcement of his appointment in June 1943, he began to contemplate a Crippsian initiative to bring Congress and Muslim League together in a national government under the existing constitution.

On 10 September Wavell raised with Amery and his Under-Secretary 'the possibility of a renewed attempt to secure a provisional government at the Centre containing the party leaders, on the main lines of the Cripps proposals': an Indian-

[1] Lord Butler, *The Art of the Possible* (1972), 111.
[2] Linlithgow to Lumley, 25 Nov. 1942, *Transfer of Power*, iii. 218.
[3] Butler to Hoare, 27 Nov. 1942, loc. cit.
[4] Butler to Hoare, 24 June 1943, Templewood Papers, XIII. 19.
[5] Wavell's Journal, 31 July 1945, P. Moon (ed.), *Wavell: The Viceroy's Journal* (1973), 159.
[6] Ibid. 19 Oct. 1943, 32–4.

ized council except for the Viceroy and Commander-in-Chief
with the Governor-General's special duties and powers remaining.[1] With Churchill absent in North America Attlee
reconstituted the India Committee, which considered the
proposals on 17 and 29 September and 4 October. Wavell
received little support.

Wavell's draft scheme contrasted stark alternatives: either
'the present policy of inaction', 'an official Government', and
and executive of 'men selected for their personal qualities'; or
the revival of the Cripps offer, a national government, and a
council 'of men selected for their representative character'
working 'in practice as a Cabinet'.[2] He sought permission to
convene a conference of political leaders to give effect to the
latter alternative, the Congress prisoners being released for
the purpose. He explained that while the plan followed the
Cripps offer in principle it did not demand the political leaders'
acceptance of the Cripps method of settling the post-war
constitution. He asked that the timing of the initiative be
left to his discretion.

Wavell won Cripps's backing and the unenthusiastic support
of Amery and Halifax (who attended the Committee meetings
by invitation).[3] Grigg opposed any approach to Congress.
Anderson thought that the plan was radical and forfeited the
advantage of Cripps's scheme—the achievement of agreement
on a constitutional settlement. Both he and Simon expected
that the Viceroy's position would be dangerously weakened.
Even Attlee was now disinclined to reform the executive by
introducing party representatives, and preferred to build up
the centre out of elements drawn from the provinces and the
Indian states. Here was the germ of a concern that later weighed
with him, the undemocratic and non-representative character
of any council formed from party oligarchies.

The product of the Committee's labours was an agreement (with Grigg dissenting) to submit to the Cabinet a
directive to Wavell far more generalized and less satisfactory
than he had sought. He was merely to be empowered, given
favourable circumstances and the prior consent of Cabinet at

1 Note of Amery–Wavell interview, [10 Sept. 1943], *Transfer of Power*, iv. 108.
2 Memo. by Viceroy-Designate for India Committee, 15 Sept. 1943, ibid. 116.
3 India Committee, 17 Sept. 1943, ibid. 120; *Wavell's Journal*, 20 Sept. 1943, 18.

the time, to consult with India's political leaders with a view to breaking the deadlock.

With a note to his colleagues on 6 October, and at a War Cabinet meeting the next day, Churchill demolished not only Wavell's proposal but also the Committee's directive. Under the strongest possible pressure from Churchill, the War Cabinet concluded: first, that no immediate course of action should be laid down; second, that the onus of disavowing 'their present attitude' should remain with Congress and there should be no negotiations with Gandhi; and third, that he, the Prime Minister, should draft a directive to Wavell.[1] The vagueness of Churchill's directive led Amery to observe to Wavell: 'You are wafted to India on a wave of hot air.'[2]

Churchill based his case upon the folly of forming a government with Gandhi and the Congress, whose every effort had recently been to undermine the war effort. 'Victory is the best foundation for great constitutional departures.'[3] Change must await its achievement. Churchill's directive entreated caution: '. . . you will beware above all things lest the achievement of victory . . . should be retarded by undue concentration on political issues while the enemy is at the gate.'[4] He was blunter in conversation: '. . . only over his dead body would any approach to Gandhi take place'.[5]

As early as July 1943 Wavell formed the view that Churchill 'hates India and everything to do with it' and agreed with Amery that he knew 'as much of the Indian problem as George III did of the American colonies'.[6] But he had been unprepared for the Cabinet's 'spinelessness, lack of interest, opportunism. . . . I have discovered that the Cabinet is not honest in its expressed desire to make progress in India; and that very few of them have any foresight or political courage.'[7] Wavell speculated that Churchill feared a division among the Conservatives over the Indian question that would destroy his

[1] Memo. by P. M., 6 Oct. 1943, *Transfer of Power*, iv. 165; War Cabinet, 7 Oct. 1943, ibid. 168.
[2] *Wavell's Journal*, 8 Oct. 1943, 23.
[3] Memo. of 6 Oct., loc. cit.
[4] Directive to Viceroy Designate, 8 Oct. 1943, *Transfer of Power*, iv. 172.
[5] *Wavell's Journal*, 8 Oct. 1942, 23.
[6] Ibid. 27 July 1943, 12.
[7] Ibid. 7 and 8 Oct. 1943, 22–3.

government. There was also the danger that a division between the parties might destroy the wartime coalition prematurely. Churchill's opponents on Indian policy had good reason to defer to his prejudices for the duration. This would help to explain Labour's unwillingness to press the issue in March 1944 when its Advisory Committee on Imperial Questions urged the creation of a national government. Wartime unity at home took precedence over an initiative for unity in India.[1]

Not until 24 October 1944, after a full year in office, did Wavell take up the constitutional problem again. He then appealed to Churchill:

... my primary reason for writing is that I feel very strongly that the future of India is the problem on which the British Commonwealth and the British reputation will stand or fall in the post-war period. To my mind, our strategic security, our name in the world for statesmanship and fair dealing, and much of our economic well-being will depend on the settlement we make in India. . . . And yet I am bound to say that after a year's experience in my present office I feel that the vital problems of India are being treated by H.M.G. with neglect, even sometimes with hostility and contempt. . . . There remains a deep sense of frustration and discontent amongst practically all educated Indians, which renders the present arrangements for government insecure and impermanent. . . . The present Government of India cannot continue indefinitely, or even for long. . . . If our aim is to retain India as a willing member of the British Commonwealth, we must make some imaginative and constructive move without delay.[2]

Wavell stressed the inevitability of negotiations with Congress and the League sooner or later. He judged the present a propitious moment, for after the war there was bound to be 'a fertile field for agitation', with the release of political prisoners, the demobilization of troops, and the closure of munitions factories.

Wavell proposed 'a provisional political Government, of the type suggested in the Cripps declaration, within the present constitution', coupled with an attempt to reach a constitutional settlement. He would begin by calling a small conference of political leaders to frame agreed proposals for the composition

[1] Report in Bevin Collection 2/11.
[2] Wavell to Churchill, 24 Oct. 1944, *Transfer of Power*, v. 64.

of the transitional government and consider the re-establish-
ment of popular governments in the provinces now under
official rule.

Churchill's brief reply, a month later, repeated his decision
of the previous year: that 'these very large problems require
to be considered at leisure and best of all in victorious peace'.[1]
Wavell, however, was not to be put off. Convinced 'that present
time is most favourable opportunity we have had for some
years to make progress with Indian problem', he intimated
to Amery that unless his recommendation received urgent
attention by the Cabinet he would seek permission to fly home
to state his case.[2]

Amery appealed to Attlee, as leader of one half of the coalition, to intercede with Churchill: '. . . we cannot possibly put
ourselves in the position to have it come out in the future
that we refused even to consider [Wavell's] proposals . . .'.[3] In
consequence, on 6 December the India Committee took up
the matter. Except for Cripps, who wanted to hear Wavell in
person, the Committee saw decisive objections to the proposed
revival of the 1942 offer. The Wavell scheme abandoned the
original requirement for a prior general agreement among the
Indian parties on the constitutional settlement. It would
destroy a sound central government and bring Gandhi to the
fore at a time when he had fallen into obscurity. It was essentially a reiteration of the September 1943 proposals and there
had been 'no such change in the Indian position as to strengthen the case for their acceptance'.[4] However, the Committee
did concede that a comprehensive and fundamental analysis
of the alternative methods of dealing with the Indian problem
was now appropriate. Wavell's scheme should be evaluated
within this broad context and should not be rejected without
him having the opportunity to argue it in person. The War
Cabinet approved these conclusions on 18 December.

Wavell's visit was put off until March. Meanwhile the
Committee traversed past statements of constitutional policy
and appraised at length a range of alternative approaches to

1 Churchill to Wavell, 26 Nov. 1944, ibid. 111.
2 Wavell to Amery, 1 Dec. 1944, ibid. 123.
3 Letter, 2 Dec. 1944, ibid. 125.
4 India Committee, 6 Dec. 1944, ibid. 137.

its fulfilment. Half of the members of the Committee believed that the expectation of transferring power to a responsible self-governing India in the early post-war period was impracticable or misguided. Simon continued to deplore the Irwin declaration of 1929 and remained incredulous that the Viceroy could be relegated to the position of a Dominion Governor-General. Amery called in question the suitability of responsible government for India and favoured an irremovable central executive. Butler envisaged a British presence for a long time to come, while Grigg thought that as twenty years would be required to Indianize the army then such was the minimum period for a full transfer of power. Still, the protracted deliberations produced no constructive alternative to Wavell's scheme. When Wavell arrived home at the end of March his scheme seemed the only alternative to inaction.

Wavell's visit dragged on for nine weeks. He had to overcome a host of objections to the revival of the short-term aspect of the Cripps offer before the Committee, and Churchill and his now Conservative caretaker Cabinet, acquiesced. Simon, Butler, Grigg, and Churchill shrank from the initiative, finally agreeing to it only in order to keep the problem of India out of the election campaign in June, and because they estimated as remote Wavell's chances of winning the support of both Congress and the League. Even those who were sympathetic to an advance feared that the reconstruction of the executive would erode the Viceroy's position and place power in the hands of undemocratic, non-representative party oligarchies. Attlee and Anderson wanted a panel of politicians elected by the central and provincial legislatures, from which Wavell would choose his council. Cripps, with some support from other members of the India Committee, felt that as reconstructing the executive would necessarily reduce the Viceroy's powers, limits to the reduction should be fixed by statute. Wavell successfully resisted such garnishing, insisting that he would remain free to select his council and retain his power to override it.

In June 1945 Wavell convened at Simla a conference of twenty-two political leaders to invite their co-operation in reconstituting the Viceroy's executive on essentially Crippsian lines. The long-term aspect of the Cripps offer remained Britain's policy, but its acceptance by the parties was not a condition of the immediate reform. One task of the new council would be to consider the means of reaching agreement on the constitutional problem.

Though Congress was prepared to enter the executive on the basis that Wavell proposed—four Hindus, four Muslims, and two of the 'minor minorities'—his initiative failed when Jinnah refused to participate unless the League nominated all of the Muslim members. In accordance with the realities of provincial politics Wavell was obliged to insist that one of the Muslims must represent the Punjab, which was governed by the Unionist Party and the non League Premier, Khizar Hyat Khan. Jinnah's strength, however, was now such that the Conservative government would never agree to the reconstruction of the central executive without his co-operation.

(iv) The Offer, Partition, and Independence

Jinnah's rejection of Wavell's scheme reflects the profound change that had overtaken Indian politics since the Cripps mission. The scheme's concession of parity of representation to Hindus and Muslims did, to a certain extent, recognize Jinnah's claim that India was two nations. His demand that the League must nominate all of the Muslim members flowed logically from his argument that the League was the authentic voice of the Muslim nation. From the time of his first proposal for an initiative in 1943 Wavell had recognized that the parties' acceptance of Cripps's post-war constitutional solution could no longer be made a condition of the reform of the executive. In November 1944 he argued the point in correspondence with R. G. Casey, Governor of Bengal, who favoured a simple revival of the Cripps offer in its entirety: 'I doubt if a mere restatement of the Cripps offer would do, as the Muslims would certainly stand out for their own idea of Pakistan, which has, I think, crystallized since the Cripps offer.'[1] Wavell hoped that the Muslims might eventually accept some loose form of Indian federation if a basis of communal co-operation could be established by their association with Hindus in the practical problems of central government during the war. Until Jinnah's rejection of the Simla scheme he did not realize that a reconstruc-

---

[1] Wavell to Casey, 13 Nov. 1944, ibid. 96.

tion of the executive that did not recognize the League's quasi-national status had become impracticable.

At the time of the Cripps mission Jinnah was prepared to commit the League to participation in central government even though the offer provided only for provinces to opt out of the Indian Union. The League was then purely a party of opposition, governing none of the Muslim majority provinces that it claimed for Pakistan. At that time Jinnah could feel no assurance that the Muslim provinces would choose to opt out of the Union, but the fact that the offer admitted Pakistan in principle was sufficient to win his co-operation.[1]

The constitutional deadlock that followed the failure of the Cripps mission gave Jinnah and the League three years in which to strengthen their organization and extend their influence. Between 1942 and 1945 the League became the party of government in Sind, Bengal, the N.W.F.P., and even the Hindu-majority province of Assam. In the latter two cases the League ruled where Congress had once governed. Of the provinces that Jinnah claimed for Pakistan only the Punjab denied him. If he had secured power there perhaps he would have accepted Wavell's scheme. Even so, he would surely have sought more than the restatement of the Cripps offer of local option. He now hoped, with some reason, for a Pakistan that included all of the Muslim majority provinces, but the League's ascendancy was too precarious for him to be confident of achieving it by plebiscite.

The total subjection of Congress for a thousand days distorted the course of Indian politics and contributed to Jinnah's unreal sense of the relative importance of the two parties. His success ensured that his claim for a separate and sovereign Muslim nation could not be denied, but once the constitutional dialogue was reopened—by Labour's Cabinet Mission in 1946 —the claim was seen to be valid for only the Muslim majority areas of the two largest Muslim provinces. The partition of Bengal and the Punjab was a logical consequence of the emergence of the League as a quasi-nation, a Muslim party of government, in the unreal political world that was ushered in by the failure of the Cripps mission.

---

[1] It is noteworthy that Cripps did amend the proposed arrangements for plebiscites to meet Jinnah's wishes (C.M., 380, 392, 393).

The defeat of the Cripps offer in 1942 was a watershed in the history of the partition of India. The offer was a Labour initiative to tackle the problem of Indian freedom with unity. It was defeated by a Conservative axis that linked the Prime Minister to the Viceroy. The one was the triumphant diehard who had, since 1931, preferred the Conservative back-benches to endorsing a modest scheme for advance in the central government of India. The other was the continuing representative of a federal solution that had been exposed as a sham. Neither was willing to recognize that the Congress electoral victory of 1937 or its successful government of most of the provinces of British India entitled it to participation, as a partner, in the central administration of India during the war. Neither had the least understanding of Nehru, India's war leader *manqué*, whom they humiliated and goaded, first into calling out the provincial ministries, and later into rebellion. Their prideful and wilful alienation of Congress nurtured Muslim nationalism. Already in the later 1930s the creation of autonomous provinces enjoying authority co-ordinate with that of the central government etched the outline of Muslim India around Sind, N.W.F.P., Bengal, and the Punjab. The indefinite postponement of national government at the centre, the removal of Congress from competition in provincial politics, and the recognition of Jinnah as the Muslim spokesman on all-India problems, encouraged and enabled the League to capture by constitutional process all but one of the component provinces of the putative Pakistan. The Cripps offer was the only wartime attempt to arrest this trend. Had it been successful, the trend might well have been countervailed, as Wavell came to appreciate, by the use of the central government as a means for Congress–League co-operation.

In the perspective of independence the Cripps offer was similarly a watershed. It was an enduring Labour achievement, looking forward to a new post-war order, a new Britain with an expanding home market in lieu of the vanishing markets of a subject empire. It was a realistic scheme to come to terms with the problems of Britain as well as the problem of India. By 1939 India had a favourable balance of trade with Britain, by 1942 she was a creditor. There was difficulty in recruiting for the Indian Civil Service and while the basis for rule with

India's consent was gone so was the will, and indeed the means, to remain by force. The commercial, military, and class pillars of British dominance were damaged beyond repair. Throughout the war the Conservatives continued to entertain fantasies of a post-war imperial presence, an empire by treaty. Even after the transformed electorate of 1945 had rejected Churchill he still wished to 'keep a bit of India'.[1]

The irony is that by the time Labour achieved office its scheme for the transfer of power was no longer feasible. For the moment the Cripps offer remained the policy of the Labour government. But by July 1945 the initiative that had originated in discussions with Nehru at Cripps's country house seven years earlier was at an end. Cripps and Attlee now needed a different solution to the Indian problem.

[1] *Wavell's Journal*, 31 Aug. 1945, 168.

INDEX

Aiyar, Sivaswami, 50
Alexander, Horace, 5, 58–9, 120, 127
Ambedkar, Dr. B. R., 60
Amery, Leopold, 31, 34, 36–7, 41, 44, 143; and Linlithgow, 32–3, 51–3, 56–8, 71, 74, 79–80, 83–4, 97, 111–12, 121, 133–4, 137; rebuked by Churchill, 35; and Cripps offer (1942), 45–6, 50, 53–7, 59–60, 63–4, 66, 68–71, 73, 76, 79–80, 92, 103, 134; and July 1942 statement of policy, 132–3; and Wavell, 138–40, 142
Anderson, Sir John, 21, 28, 41, 53, 56–7, 59, 63, 79, 139, 143
Aney, Dr. M. S., 120
Asaf Ali, 39, 84, 98
Atlantic Charter, 42–3, 49
Attlee, Clement Richard, 147; and 1935 scheme, 2, 23 n. 1; criticizes Linlithgow, 7, 79; and first offer, 34, 41; as member of the Cabinet, 58–9, 63; his Indian situation memorandum, 55–7; and Cripps offer (1942), 47, 51, 53–4, 57, 66; and Wavell's India policy, 139, 142–3
Azad, Maulana Abul Kalam
   and Cripps, 13, 15, 106, 112, 114, 124; and Linlithgow, 33, 46; and Cripps offer (1942), 82, 84, 86, 89–91, 93–5, 98, 102–3, 106, 110, 114, 124–5, 127–9; invitation to meet Wavell, 94, 98; and Johnson, 106, 110

Bajpai, Sir Girja Shankar, 48, 104
Balfour, Lord, 9
Barnes, Leonard, 4
Benn, Wedgwood, 8, 31, 46
Berle, A. A., 48–9, 62, 104, 131
Bevan, Aneurin, 4
Bevin, Ernest, 41, 46–7, 56
Birla, G. D., 11–12, 124
Bracken, Brendan, 138
Butler, R. A., 8–9, 70–1, 73, 134, 137–8, 143

Cabinet Mission, 12 n. 1, 145
Cadogan, Sir Edward, 45, 57, 70–1

Casey, R. G., 144
Chamberlain, Neville, 21, 24–5, 28, 34
Chiang Kai-shek, Generalissimo, 61–2
Churchill, Winston Spencer
   and India Act (1935), 1, 4; and first offer, 21, 23, 25, 28, 34–6, 40–4, 59; forms government, 31; Atlantic Charter speech, 42–3, 49; and Cripps offer (1942), 45, 47, 50–1, 53, 57–8, 62, 66, 69–70, 73–8, 85, 89, 93–7, 99–101, 111, 114–19, 121–3, 126–7, 130, 134; discusses Indian reforms with Roosevelt, 47, 49–50, 69, 73, 105, 117, 130–1; his do-nothing policy, 136–8, 140–3, 146; and 1945 election, 147
civil disobedience
   1929–31 movement, 21; threat of, 24, 28, 31, 38; and Gandhi, 37; rejected at Wardha (1940), 39; sanctioned by the A.I.C.C., 135–6
Congress, Indian National
   and federation, 2–3; 1937 election success, 2–3, 6, 146; and Muslim League, 2, 11–14, 16–17, 22, 25, 27; All-India Congress Committee, 36–7, 40, 135–6; Working Committee, 3, 5, 7, 30, 38–40, 50, 88, 93–5, 98–9, 110–13, 115, 125–8, 132, 134, 136; resignation of provincial ministries, 7, 16, 20, 23, 38; and Cripps scheme, 11, 13–14; and first offer, 19–23, 25–6, 28–33, 38–40, 53; Ramgarh resolution, 30, 38; and Revolutionary Movements Ordinance, 31, 37–8; Wardha discussions, 38–40; policy of co-operation, 38–40, 50–1; rejects Gandhi's non-violence for national defence, 39–40, 50, 93, 128; and Churchill's scheme, 58; and Cripps offer (1942), 82, 84, 87–96, 98–9, 107–12, 115, 119–20, 122–30, 134–5; rejects Cripps offer, 120, 125, 127–8, 130–1; Quit India campaign, 132, 135; and Wavell's policy, 138, 141, 143–4